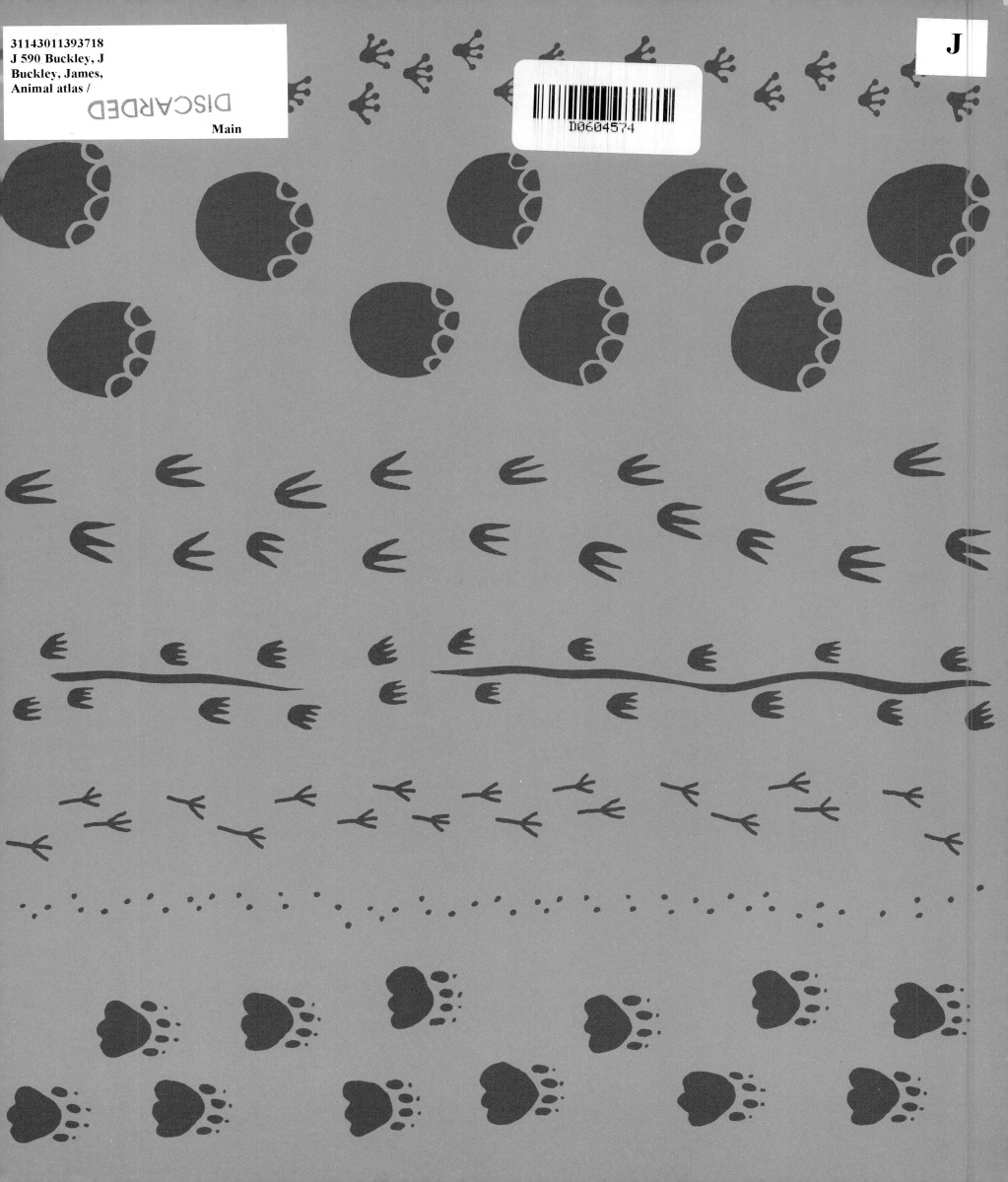

J

animal atlas

Text by James Buckley, Jr.

Maps by Aaron Meshon

LIBERTY
STREET

Executive Editor: **Beth Sutinis**
Project Editor: **Deirdre Langeland**
Art Director: **Georgia Morrissey**
Project Manager: **Stephanie Braga**
Associate Prepress Manager: **Alex Voznesenskiy**

Produced by
Shoreline Publishing Group LLC
Santa Barbara, CA
Editorial Director **James Buckley Jr.**
Special thanks to animal experts Robert Timm (University of
Kansas); Ian Recchio (herpetological curator); Brendan Dunphy
(Iowa State University); Nancy McToldridge (Santa Barbara Zoo);
and Scott Simon (University of California, Santa Barbara).
The producer also thanks the excellent folks at Liberty Street for
their help in making this cool book!

Published by Liberty Street, an imprint of Time Inc. Books
225 Liberty Street
New York, New York 10281

LIBERTY STREET is a trademark of Time Inc.

ISBN 10: 1-61893-165-2
ISBN 13: 978-1-61893-165-8
Library of Congress Control Number: 2015959681

First edition, 2016

1 TLF 16

10 9 8 7 6 5 4 3 2 1

Time Inc. Books products may be purchased for business or
promotional use. For information on bulk purchases, please contact
Ilene Schreider in the Special Sales Department at (212) 522-3985.

To order Time Inc. Books Collector's Editions, please call (800) 327-
6388, Monday through Friday, 7 a.m.-9 p.m., Central Time.

We welcome your comments and suggestions about Time Inc. Books.
Please write to us at:
Time Inc. Books
Attention: Book Editors
P.O. Box 62310
Tampa, Florida 33662-2310

timeincbooks.com

🌐 CONTENTS

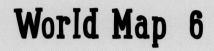

INTRODUCTION

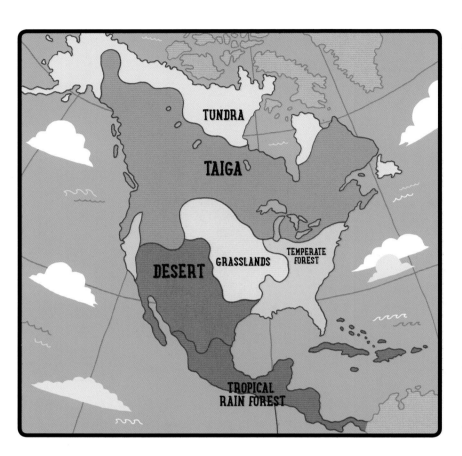

In most atlases, the maps show countries or groups of countries. The lines on those maps mark borders, showing where one nation stops and another begins. The maps in this book are a little different. They show the borders of the major biomes of the world. A biome is defined by its temperature, vegetation, terrain, and rainfall. By visiting the major biomes on each of the seven continents, you'll get to know what they look, feel, and sound like, and meet some of the many animals that live there.

ROAR

People are the dominant species on the planet. That makes it our job to keep our shared home safe for animals of all kinds. As we have spread around the world, we have done some things that have hurt animals. Stories in this ROAR box show how people are trying to make life better and safer for animals of all kinds.

Surprisingly Human

Look for these boxes to find out how animals are, in some ways, a lot like us! Do we share physical traits? Do we have similar behaviors? Humans are animals, too, of course, so this feature connects us in other ways.

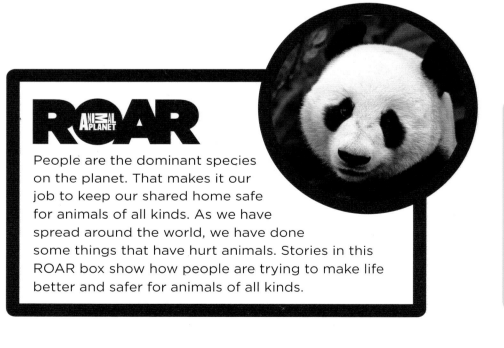

WHAT IS A BIOME?

If you traveled across a continent, you would likely pass through several biomes. Each biome would be quite different from the others, but would share important features with examples of the same biome on other continents. A grassland in Asia is similar, for example, to a grassland in North America. Both get about the same amount of rainfall, have similar plants, and the same temperatures throughout the year. Here's a look at the features of each of the biomes covered in this atlas.

ALPINE

Named for the high mountains in central Europe called the Alps, this biome has tall peaks, steep slopes, and high meadows. Alpine biomes are often cold and sometimes freezing, with very few plants outside their forested areas.

DESERT

Dry, dry, dry: That's a desert. This biome gets very little rain (less than 10 inches/25.4 cm a year), so few plants grow there. The ground is dirt, sand, or rough rocks. The temperature can be very hot in the day, but cold at night.

MARINE

"Marine" means having to do with the water, so these biomes include oceans, large lakes, or river systems. This is the only biome that is completely underwater.

GRASSLANDS

Wide, low-lying areas of grass are typical of this biome. Different grasslands have different types of grasses (and different names), but all have four seasons and large, open areas.

RAINFOREST

A wet region with at least 65 inches (165 cm) of rain a year, a rainforest has thick, heavy plants, often including tall trees, exotic flowers, and vines. It never freezes, and temperatures are very warm.

TEMPERATE FOREST

This biome experiences all four seasons. Many of the trees are deciduous, which means they lose their leaves in winter. Other trees can be evergreen. These forests often include ponds, lakes, and rivers, too. Many plants grow easily, offering homes for millions of animals.

TUNDRA

The areas of the globe closest to the North Pole are bleak, cold, and desolate. The ground is frozen for nearly the entire year. Tundra can include high mountain peaks or rough hills. There is very little plant life—just mosses and low grass—but animals manage to find ways to live there.

TAIGA

Below the northern tundra line, the taiga (TIE-gah) stretches around the globe, covered in most areas by huge forests. Most of the trees there are evergreens. Some areas of the taiga include marshes. The taiga freezes in the winter, but thaws in spring, meaning many animals there hibernate until the weather improves.

WORLD MAP

Most of the Earth's land is divided into the seven continents, and each of the seven continents includes a wide range of biomes. The animals pictured on this map represent just a few of the millions of species that live in them. You can look for your favorites and jump forward to the continent that they live on, or read page-by-page to discover new places and animals.

At the beginning of each chapter you will find another map that shows the major biomes on that continent, and meet the special passport animal that will be your guide. Read on to learn more about the biomes, and to get to know some of the animals that live in each one.

MEET YOUR TRAVEL GUIDES!

On every continent, you will meet a special tour guide. Each of these animals lives in many places on its home continent. They will chime in with tidbits, insider info, and trivia about some of the other animals you'll meet.

Giant Asian Mantis
ASIA

African Elephant
AFRICA

European Tree Frog
EUROPE

American Robin
NORTH AMERICA

Marine Iguana
SOUTH AMERICA

Tasmanian Devil
AUSTRALIA

Chinstrap Penguin
ANTARCTICA

ARCTIC OCEAN

NORTH AMERICA

ATLAN
OCEA

SOUTH AMERI

EUROPE

ASIA

PACIFIC OCEAN

AFRICA

INDIAN OCEAN

AUSTRALIA

SOUTHERN OCEAN

ANTARCTICA

TUNDRA

TAIGA

GRASSLANDS

DESERT

TEMPERATE FOREST

ALPINE

RAINFOREST

🌐 ASIA

Asia is by far the largest of the seven continents. So it's not surprising that it also contains a great number of different biomes. From the frozen lands at the far north, through high mountains and desolate deserts, all the way south to some of the world's densest rainforests—Asia has it all! It also has the most people (more than 4 billion!), but in areas west and north of China, the population is less than 10 people per square mile. With that much open space, there is room for a wealth of animals.

Passenger Information

NAME: GIANT ASIAN MANTIS
SCIENTIFIC NAME: *Hierodula membranacea*
SIZE: 3-4 inches (7-10 cm)
ADDRESS: Southeast Asia
FAVORITE MEAL: Insects, small reptiles

— 27 —

Visas

This mantis blends into the trees and vegetation of rainforests or temperate forests. Unlike some species, they don't wait around for food to wander by. They use their strong back legs to leap and attack and their lightning-fast front legs to snatch. From insects to small reptiles to birds—if they catch it, they eat it.

— 28 —

LANDS AND ISLANDS

Asia's enormous rainforest biome stretches across the southeast mainland and spills onto thousands of islands. On the mainland and the islands, animals make their homes amid tall trees and thick vegetation, or in dark, dense soil on the forest floor. These hard-to-reach areas are home to many plant and animal species that humans still have never seen!

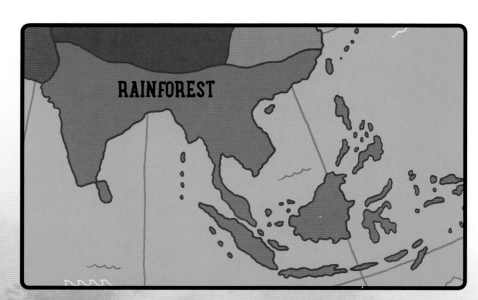

RAINFOREST

Open wide! Organutans have 32 teeth, just like humans. Of course, I don't have any!

ORANGUTAN

At more than 200 pounds (90 kg), this is the world's largest tree-living mammal. The orangutan, whose name means "person of the forest" in Malay, is the only great ape found in Asia. Orangutans are very intelligent. They have been seen using large tree leaves as umbrellas in the rain.

KOMODO DRAGON

The world's largest lizard lives at the top of the food chain on several Indonesian islands. Its forked tongue seeks out the scent of prey. The dragon can move fast enough to catch larger mammals and birds. A strong bite with sharp teeth makes the kill.

LEAF INSECT

Does this look like a plant to you? Look again! That's an insect with some amazing camouflage. With an exoskeleton that mimics nearby leaf patterns, the leaf insect is able to hide while it seeks the leaves and plants it likes to eat.

SLOW LORIS

Lorises' excellent night vision and great sense of smell help them find food at night. They eat fruit, insects, and bird eggs. After catching an insect, they can hang upside down and eat! During the day, they sleep curled up into a tight ball.

FORMOSA TOAD

A mottled skin pattern helps this toad hide among the leaves on the forest floor, avoiding predators and waiting for prey. Its name comes from an old name for its home, Taiwan.

SUMATRAN RHINOCEROS

Its home today is on only two islands (Sumatra and Borneo), but this two-horned rhino used to roam southern Asia. In 2015, they were declared extinct on the island of Malaysia. It is among the most threatened rhino species, with fewer than 100 left alive.

The rainforest home of all these animals is under threat from many directions. The trees are being cut by loggers and by companies looking for valuable palm oil. More than 3 million acres (1.2 million hectare) of forest on the mainland and on the islands are disappearing every year. Many groups are working with governments and local farmers to find new ways to preserve this important and incredibly diverse part of the world.

Surprisingly Human

Do you ever "start your day with a song"? Silvery gibbon females do that every day. Each female "vocalizes," or makes a music-like sound that tells other gibbons to stay out of her territory. The call can be heard for a mile!

Like most snakes, cobras don't have eyelids. They sleep with their eyes open. A see-through scale called a brille protects their eyes.

KING COBRA

At up to 18 feet (5.4 m) long, this is one of the longest venomous snakes in the world. Cobras often live in forested areas near towns and villages, where they can encounter humans. When a cobra feels threatened by a human or other animal, and it cannot escape, it flattens its neck into a "hood," and hisses in an attempt to scare the other animal away. If that fails, they will bite—they kill many people each year.

SILVERY GIBBON
These small apes spend their whole lives in the treetops, almost never going to the forest floor. They move from tree to tree in search of ripening fruit.

WAGLER'S PIT VIPER
Snakes in the trees? That's right, this viper lives and hunts among the branches. Part of its name comes from small pits on its face that help it sense heat from prey.

PROBOSCIS MONKEY
These endangered monkeys are famous for their tremendous noses. Even though they spend most of their lives in trees, they are also among the best swimmers in the forest.

RED CENTIPEDE
The name of this 6-inch (15 cm) arthropod means "100 feet." They don't really have that many—usually about 40— but they do have a nasty venom that can make a person sick. They are predators, eating just about anything in their path.

BIRD OF PARADISE
In the dark green of the rainforest, the colorful feathers of the bird of paradise stand out. The male birds of more than 30 species flash their colors to attract mates.

GOLDEN WEB SPIDER
This spider's webbing is so strong that people are sometimes able to turn abandoned webs into fishing nets. The spider has been known to trap birds, though it doesn't eat them.

13

RED PANDA

Red pandas eat bamboo and plants in forest homes in south Asia. They forage at night to avoid predators, but can also protect themselves with claws and a stinky odor. These cat-sized animals are distantly related to the giant panda.

BEARDED VULTURE

This raptor takes its common name from the feathers on its neck. It eats mostly bones. To get at the tasty inside parts, it drops the bones from great heights, then swoops down to peck at the pieces with its hooked beak.

HIMALAYAN AGAMA

The cold-blooded agama seeks out sunny rocks to keep itself warm in the chilly foothills of the Himalayas. This insect-eating animal can only stay outside in the summer, however, and spends most of the winter hibernating.

BHARAL

Bharals are also known as blue sheep. They have great balance and can live and eat on steep, rocky slopes. To hide from their main predator, the snow leopard, bharals can hold very still and blend in with the rocks, as shown in the bottom photo.

YAK

Like their cousins the cows, yaks have been put to work by farmers for thousands of years. At high elevations, the air is thinner, making it harder to breathe. Yaks have much bigger lungs than cows, so they can breathe in the mountains.

Those feathers did not grow orange. This bird rubs dirt on them to look more impressive!

TOP OF THE WORLD

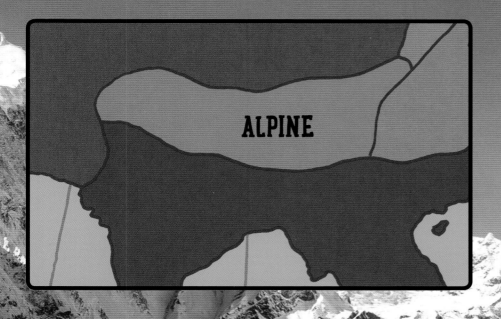

ALPINE

The Himalayas, the highest mountains on Earth, tower over central Asia. Many are more than 20,000 feet (6,096 m) high. Few creatures can live at the highest points, where the weather can be deadly cold year round. But the foothills below the towering peaks, where the climate is warmer, are home to a surprising number of animals. Those animals live in meadows, small areas of forest, and on rocky slopes.

SNOW LEOPARD

Every part of this endangered animal helps it survive in cold, snowy lands. Its wide nose heats up cold air before the air can hurt the animal's lungs. Huge paws won't sink into soft snow. A thick coat of fur keeps the leopard warm, while helping it blend into the background. Powerful legs give it the ability to pounce on prey, including the bharal.

SAND AND SCRUB

The vast Gobi Desert in Central Asia (center of map) connects to the Arabian desert (bottom left of map). Together, they form an enormous but very dry and sandy biome. In a land with little rainfall, animals have to be extra hardy to survive. These animals each have adaptations that give them the tools to find food, water, and shelter in lands where people can rarely live for long.

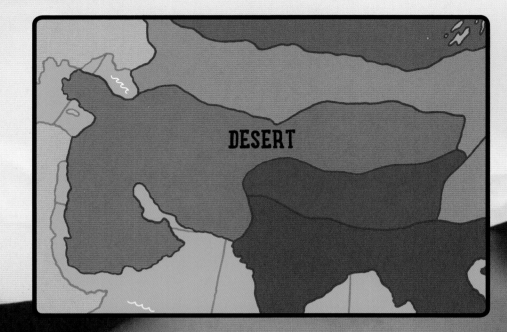

DESERT

ORNATE SPINY-TAILED LIZARD

Lizards need the sun to keep warm, so the desert is the perfect home for this 16-inch (40-cm) reptile. It eats small plants and seeds that it finds in the scrubby ground, and will sometimes eat insects. Ornate means very fancy or decorated, which describes the colorful scale patterns of male ornate spiny-tailed lizards.

PLATE-TAILED GECKO

To escape the extremes of hot and cold in the desert, these lizards live most of their lives underground. They come out to hunt insects. This gecko gets its name from large, plate-like scales that cover the top of its tail.

DESERT JERBOA

These tiny rodents need those long legs and big ears to help them escape from their key predator, the golden eagle (see below). Jerboas get all their water from the plants and insects they eat. That comes in handy in a place like the Gobi, which might only get an average of 7 inches (17.7 cm) of rain in a year.

GOLDEN EAGLE

High above the sands and grasslands of central Asia, the golden eagle floats, looking for prey far below. Like all raptors, it uses excellent eyesight to spot prey, then swoops down to grab it with its sharp talons. In this area, nomadic Kazakh hunters (inset) carry on a centuries-old tradition. They train the eagles to hunt with them, sending them out to bring back mink, polecats, rabbits, and other small mammals.

DESERT RED FOX

Foxes live in many places around the world. This species has adapted well to life in the desert. Fur between its toes acts like socks to keep its feet from the hot sands. Large ears help listen for predators, but can also be used to release heat from the fox's body. Its coloring is also good desert camouflage.

Eagles trained as hunters only work for a few years. Then they are released back into the wild to hunt on their own!

ROAR ANIMAL PLANET

The desert can be a hard place for animals to live. When humans get in the way, it can be even harder. Some desert species have been hunted into extinction. Others are threatened as their food sources disappear. Some habitats can even be wrecked by off-road driving. Several countries in this area, including Saudi Arabia, Jordan, and the United Arab Emirates, have created large preserves to help animals and plants survive unharmed.

EUROPEAN SOUSLIK

Because of the way these little rodents look and act, sousliks are sometimes called European ground squirrels. They have a similar body type to a squirrel, but they live in underground dens instead of trees. They come out during the day to find nuts, seeds, and berries to eat.

SAIGA ANTELOPE

Dusty summers on the steppe make breathing hard for large animals. Saiga antelopes use a nose flap to clear away the dust. In the spring, huge herds of them migrate north. Saiga antelope populations have plummeted from more than a million in the 1950s to less than 100,000 today.

PYGMY HOG

Scientists thought this 1-foot (.3 m) animal was extinct in the 1960s. After a few wild ones were found, conservation efforts have helped the population grow. Pygmy hogs are still very rare and live mostly in northern India, where the steppe biome merges into lower foothills.

Surprisingly Human

Have you ever walked single file? On a field trip, perhaps, with the teacher in front and kids following? That's how pygmy hogs move through the brush, with mom leading the way and piglets lining up behind.

SOCIABLE LAPWING

This bird got its name from the enormous flocks in which it migrated. However, the size of those flocks has shrunk dramatically. Scientists are not really sure why that is happening. Are the birds' breeding grounds turning to farmland? Are the birds being hunted? Lapwings often migrate from their homes in central Asia to spend winter in warmer places such as Israel or India.

ROAR

Pandas don't live on the steppes, but their only remaining home is just to the east in China. They live only in hilly, bamboo forests there—but we wanted to make sure they were in the ANIMAL ATLAS! The Chinese government has a very active program to help pandas. Pandas born at zoos around the world usually end up returning to China. Large, protected reserves in China keep pandas safe, too.

GIANT STEPPES

The wide meadows and grasslands of Central Asia are known as the "steppes." These regions experience very cold winters and hot and dry summers. Because of the steppes' location in the center of the continent, people have been crisscrossing there for thousands of years. Nomadic tribes once dominated the land, but empire after empire has swept through to conquer. Some permanent human development has been built, but it's such a large area, animals usually have plenty of room to roam.

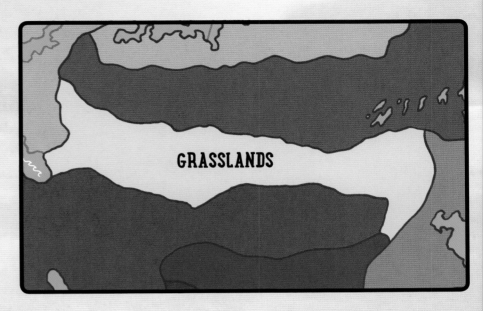

GRASSLANDS

Shh! Don't tell this eagle there is a souslik on the other page. Rodents like that are its favorite prey!

EASTERN IMPERIAL EAGLE

With a wingspan of more than six feet (0.6 m), this impressive raptor soars high above the steppes. Some live their whole lives here, nesting and breeding. Others migrate to warmer areas in winter. Like many large birds, these eagles mate for life, staying with the same mate year after year. They make their nests in the tallest trees they can find.

ROLLING CHINA

Thanks in part to plentiful rainfall and a milder climate, a large forested area grows in eastern Asia and on parts of Japan. The area experiences four seasons, but winters and summers are not as harsh or extreme as in the steppes or mountains. Many areas are heavily populated by people, but where wild areas remain, animals have found homes amid the trees, meadows, and fields.

TEMPERATE FOREST

No one would ever want to use my exoskeleton for a winter coat!

SABLE

The thick, soft coat of this member of the weasel family helps keep it warm in winter. That coat has been very popular in human clothing, too. Sables were heavily hunted for centuries. Today, most sables that are used in clothing are raised on farms. In the wild, sables are carnivores, eating mice and voles.

CHINESE GORAL

Less than 3 feet (1 m) tall, gorals are related to goats and have short, cone-shaped horns. They can be gray or brown. One nickname for them? The Chinese unicorn. Gorals live mostly in the higher parts of this region, feeding on grasses.

BROWN EARED PHEASANT

This is the only bird native to this area in China. They are very rare and several special preserves have been set aside to give them a safe place to live and find the seeds, insects, and berries they eat. They have a long, high-pitched call that can go on for more than a minute.

RED-CROWNED CRANE

Where water is found in the forests and fields, you'll find cranes. They wade in the shallows of marshes, ponds, and rivers to catch fish, using their long beaks. Cranes are part of many folktales in China and Japan.

NORTH COLD

The northern reaches of Asia break up into two biomes. The taiga includes the giant forests of Siberia. They are remote and almost free of people. The tundra starts where the ground is frozen year-round. The lands of the tundra are even more desolate and barren.

TUNDRA

TAIGA

FISCHER'S EIDER

Also known as the spectacled eider, this duck species lives in and near the sea. It makes its nests on shore and dives for crabs and mollusks in the ocean.

REINDEER

Wide, sharp hooves help reindeer move through thick snow and dig into snow for lichens to eat. While other species of deer have bare skin patches on their noses, reindeer have furry noses to keep them warm in extreme cold. No Santa jokes, please!

NORTHERN HAWK OWL

Hawk owls get their name because they fly like hawks, with wide sweeping flaps, hovering over prey that mostly includes lemmings and voles. Feathers that grow over their legs and feet help them stay warm in the taiga.

ELK (MOOSE)

Called elk in Eurasia but known as moose in North America, these are some of the largest forest animals around, standing as much as seven feet (2.1 m) tall and weighing 1,500 pounds (680 kg) Their velvet-covered antlers grow each year and are then shed.

SUMATRAN TIGER

Animal Facts

COMMON NAME: Sumatran tiger
SCIENTIFIC NAME: *Panthera tigris sumatrae*
LENGTH: 8 feet (4 m)
WEIGHT: 300 pounds (136 kg)
HABITAT: Wooded areas
DIET: Mammals, reptiles, fish

Where does it live?

These tigers live alone, except to mate. They each have a territory in the forested areas on this island in Indonesia, making their homes in the thick vegetation on the ground.

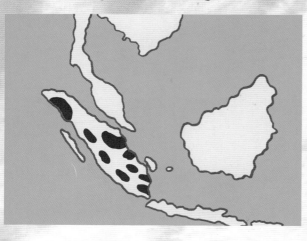

Why does it live there?

The forest provides the tiger with camouflage for tracking its prey, along with habitats for that prey.

What does it eat?

Tigers hunt mammals for the most part—pigs, deer, or boar—but will also eat fish or track down larger birds.

ROAR

This is one of the rarest animals in the world. Only about 400 Sumatran tigers exist in the wild. Others live in zoos in breeding programs. Why so rare? Their skins were very valuable and they were overhunted. Their forest habitat was also reduced dramatically by farming and logging. Several protected areas on Sumatra were formed to help give the tigers a safer home. Cameras hidden in the woods help experts track the big cats.

Animal Close Up

Tigers swim well, something most cats—big or small—don't like to do. They keep their heads out of the water as they paddle with their wide, thick paws. They cross rivers or streams to track their prey.

The familiar orange-and-black striped face of a tiger peers out at the only animals on the planet that can help it survive—you. Wildlife experts are trying to double world tiger populations by 2022.

🌐 AFRICA

Africa is the world's second largest continent, and home to some of the most famous animals on the planet. Lions, elephants, hippos, and even great white sharks call Africa home. Many of Africa's biomes are very hot, thanks to Africa's position on and near the Equator. In fact, its northern deserts are some of the hottest places on Earth. The central African rainforest is wet and steamy. Even in the parts of the continent that are farthest from the Equator, like South Africa, winters are mild.

ANIMAL ANIMAL PLANET PASSPORT

Passenger Information

NAME: **AFRICAN ELEPHANT**
SCIENTIFIC NAME: *Loxodonta africana*
HEIGHT: 8-13 feet (2.5-4 m)
ADDRESS: Savanna and forests
FAVORITE MEAL: Grasses, plants

— 27 —

Visas

Huge ears flapping and trunk waving, the mighty elephant is the largest land animal in the world. Elephants live in herds, tramping across the dusty savanna. Sadly, they are disappearing because hunters kill them for their ivory tusks. Many groups are fighting for the elephants, however, so let's trumpet that news!

— 28 —

FLIC-FLAC SPIDER

Most spiders just walk on their eight legs. This type of huntsman spider in Morocco flips over and over like a gymnast to escape predators.

ADDAX

The addax is a type of antelope that once lived in enormous herds across North Africa. However, these animals have been so hunted that they are now "critically endangered." They have to wander quite far to find plants to eat. Addax have adapted to desert life by rarely needing to drink water.

PIN-TAILED WHYDAH

Now those are some impressive tail feathers! Males of this species have black tail feathers that grow as much as 8 inches (20 cm) during the mating season. That's twice as long as the bird's whole body. They hover in the air above females, showing off!

Surprisingly Human

Human babies grow inside their mothers for about nine months—same with addax babies (though, of course, they are inside addax moms!). Addax mothers have one offspring at a time and stay with their young for almost a year after birth.

NILE MONITOR

Throughout Africa, this very large (7-foot/2.3 m) reptile finds its prey—fish, lizards, snakes, eggs, and small mammals. It is named for the Nile River, which flows through the eastern Sahara Desert in Egypt and other countries.

Vipers like this one have two hollow fangs. Their venom goes through the fangs and into their prey. Ouch!

DWARF ADDER

This snake from Africa's southwestern desert is a sidewinder, which means it can move through soft desert sands with a twisting, sideways motion. Though it eats mostly lizards, this snake's venom could harm a person.

SAHARA!

The world's largest desert stretches across the width of northern Africa. With temperatures rising well above 100°F (38°C) during the day (and plunging to near freezing at night) and water very, very hard to find, the Sahara is a brutal place to live. Yet animals of all sorts have evolved ways to deal with the desert conditions. They live mostly around the rare small areas of vegetation, but have to trek through the sand dunes to move from place to place. Humans rarely live in these dry places, as most cities and towns are near the Mediterranean coastline. The rest is for the animals.

DESERT

CAMEL

The camel's ability to go weeks without water makes it the perfect desert animal. People have used camels for centuries to carry cargo and passengers, as well as for meat and hides. The one-hump African camels are called dromedaries (a two-humped version lives in Asia). Camels also have a third eyelid. They can close that eyelid to protect their eyes, but still see through it!

THE KING'S DOMAIN

The enormous grasslands of Africa—known as the savanna—stretch for so many miles and include so many amazing animals, we gave them four pages! The savanna provides food and shelter for predator and prey alike. Though the savanna is mostly dry, seasonal rainstorms cause many species to migrate to watering holes and life-giving rivers. In many nations in central and southern Africa, wildlife preserves help protect these important lands and the threatened inhabitants.

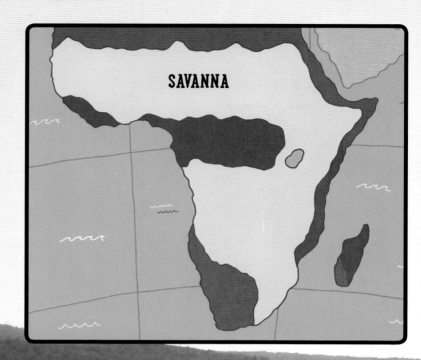

SAVANNA

LION

"The King of the Beasts" is the top predator on the savanna because it stands atop the food web. Male lions lead prides of a dozen or more females and cubs, dominating their territory with strength and their famous roar. The female lions, however, do most of the hunting, tracking down everything from mice to giraffes.

HIPPOPOTAMUS

Hippos are big (3,500 pounds/1,587 kg), loud (they snort and bellow), and very, very wet. Hippos spend most of the day in rivers and come on land at night to feed on grasses and fruits. When they are out of the water, their skin oozes a blood-red goo that acts like sunscreen. On trails at night, they can be very dangerous to humans.

Thanks to a special reflex, hippos can sleep underwater! Their brain reminds them to pop up every few minutes for a breath!

CHEETAH

Powerful legs and a flexible spine help this fast cat reach speeds of 70 miles (113 km) per hour for short distances. No prey animal can outrun them! Cheetahs rest in tall grass looking for prey. Then they stalk the prey slowly and burst out with a sprinter's speed.

Surprisingly Human

Check out your fingernails. Run your hands through your hair. You've just touched a rhino horn! Okay, not really, but stuff called keratin is what makes up our hair and nails—and also forms the rhino's famous horns.

RHINOCEROS

At more than 5,000 pounds (2,267 kg), rhinos that live in Africa are second behind only elephants as the world's largest land animals. Rhinos are herbivores. Their only real threat comes from humans, who hunt them for their horns, which are sold on the black market. Sadly, rhinos are disappearing fast.

AFRICAN ROCK PYTHON

At up to 20 feet long, this is the largest species of snake in Africa. This python doesn't inject venom into its prey, like vipers do. Instead, it just squeezes until the prey dies. That prey includes everything from small rodents to large mammals such as baby wildebeest. It has been blamed for some human deaths, too.

ZEBRA

What's black-and-white and runs all over the Savanna? The zebra! Its striped coloring helps it blend into the grasslands. And when a herd of zebras gathers, such as near a watering hole, the stripes confuse predators, who are unable to pick out a single zebra to attack.

DUNG BEETLE

The millions of animals that travel across the savanna leave behind a lot of poop. The dung beetle is there to help. These insects roll balls of animal waste and lay their eggs inside dung balls. As scavengers, they play an important role in the life cycle of the African grasslands.

GIRAFFE

Its long neck and mottled fur pattern make the giraffe one of the savanna's most recognizable animals. With a neck that can be more than 6 feet long, giraffes evolved to feed on leaves in tall trees that grow there. A giraffe's fur pattern is like our fingerprints, with no two animals exactly matching.

AFRICAN HELMETED TURTLE

These turtles live in or near water. In dry seasons, some species bury themselves in the mud of dried-up watering holes and hibernate. Other species move from pond to pond, following the water. They are omnivores, eating plants as well as fish and insects.

ROAR

Because the savanna crosses more than a dozen African countries, there is no one overall conservation project. However, in each country groups are working hard to maintain wildlife preserves, protect animals from poaching, and spread the word about this amazing place. Tourists go on safaris to see the animals in the wild and return home, organizers hope, with a new view of the importance of saving the Savanna. If you want to help, go online and read about African conservation groups like African Wildlife Conservation or the Wildlife Conservation Society.

SAVANNA BIRDS

The savanna provides many places for birds to eat and nest. Many species make their homes there at least part of the year. The grey-crowned crane (left) is now endangered. Drought and human land use have cut into their habitat. The shoebill (center) uses its large beak to snag fish from rivers and marshes. The ostrich (right) is the largest bird in the world—and the fastest feathered runner. It cannot fly, but it can run more than 30 miles (48 km) per hour.

WILDEBEEST

This one animal is part of a herd of more than a million that tramples across the savanna each year. When their grassland home dries out, they head for areas where it is raining. The migration is one of the largest in the world. On the way, the animals face danger from predators such as lions and crocodiles.

Did you know this animal is also called a gnu? Or should I say "Did you gnu"?

A JUNGLE IN HERE

Along the Equator in Africa is a fertile region of tropical rainforests. Being near the Equator means this biome has consistently hot weather. Winds and ocean currents mean that it's often rainy and wet, too. That results in amazing plant life: thick vegetation, tall trees, vines, and much more. In that lush land—and in rainforests along the Indian Ocean and on Madagascar—millions of animals make their homes.

RAINFOREST

MOUNTAIN GORILLA

Thanks to the efforts of the late zoologist Dian Fossey and others, this rare species of ape is on a slow comeback. They live only in a small area of forested hills in central Africa. They were hunted to fewer than 1,000 gorillas, but conservation efforts are helping these plant-eating animals more and more. Adult males are called "silverbacks" because their hair turns gray as they age.

DRIVER ANTS

When this army of ants goes on a march, nothing can get in its way. In central Africa, these ants swarm in groups of hundreds of thousands, overwhelming other insects, small reptiles, and even small mammals, in their search for food.

GREY PARROT

This bird's ability to mimic human and other animal sounds makes it a popular pet. But its real home is the treetops of the African rainforest. Parrots use their sharp, pointed beaks to break open nuts and fruit, their preferred foods.

GUNTHER'S SPINY LIZARD

Look! Up in the sky! It's a . . . lizard? This reptile can uses its wide body and long tail to help it glide from tree to tree. It's using gravity to get to where it wants to go!

RING-TAILED LEMUR

The African island nation of Madagascar is home to the continent's other major rainforest. Groups of these fun and frisky lemurs live amid the treetops there, looking for ripe fruit and insects to eat. However, they are omnivores, so they will also eat spiders and caterpillars, too.

MOSQUITO

This tiny, buzzing beast is the world's deadliest animal. By passing along disease agents that cause malaria, mosquitoes make hundreds of thousands of people sick every year. Many of those people live in Africa.

More than 60 species of lemurs live on Madagascar. Scientists believe there are more species to be found!

LOGGERHEAD

These sea turtles have nesting sites on Africa's Indian Ocean coast (along with other places around the world). The females return to the same beaches each year to lay their eggs. Adults then swim away, leaving the babies to make their own way in the big ocean.

SEA BASS

European sea bass are a big part of the seafood diet of people around the Mediterranean Sea. Off the coast of Tunisia, for example, sea bass is grown in pens for sale to market.

MASKED BUTTERFLY FISH

The warm waters of the Red Sea are home to several large reefs, which are the perfect habitat for these and many other colorful fish. They find their food amid the rocks and coral.

ROCK LOBSTER

Also known as spiny lobsters (or "kreef," in South Africa), these crustaceans live in underwater kelp forests around southern Africa. They eat sea urchins, mussels, crabs, and fish. Because they were being overfished, local governments now limit how many can be caught each year.

YELLOWFIN

These large tuna are some of the ocean's most long-distance travelers. Schools of tuna often cross the Atlantic between Africa and North America. They can grow to more than 400 pounds (181 kg)!

Loggerheads are one of the few animals that are not bothered by the poison of jellyfish, their favorite food.

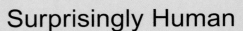

Surprisingly Human

What do you do when you see something scary? You scream, right? Lobsters can't scream, but they can make a loud scratching sound by rubbing their antennae with one of their legs. It scares off fish with a taste for lobster!

BEAUTY AND DANGER

Africa, like almost every other continent, is surrounded by water. In those waters lives an incredible variety of marine life. In the warm Mediterranean and Red Seas, reef fish thrive. To the east, the Indian Ocean is home to fish, turtles, and more. West Africa is bordered by the wild and stormy Atlantic Ocean. And lurking around South Africa is the mightiest hunter in the sea.

GREAT WHITE SHARK

At the top of the marine food web is the mighty great white, which can be 20 feet (6 m) long and weigh 1,500 pounds (680 kg). They are frequently seen in the waters off South Africa. They do most of their hunting underwater where they go after seals and penguins, but have been seen breaching, as shown here.

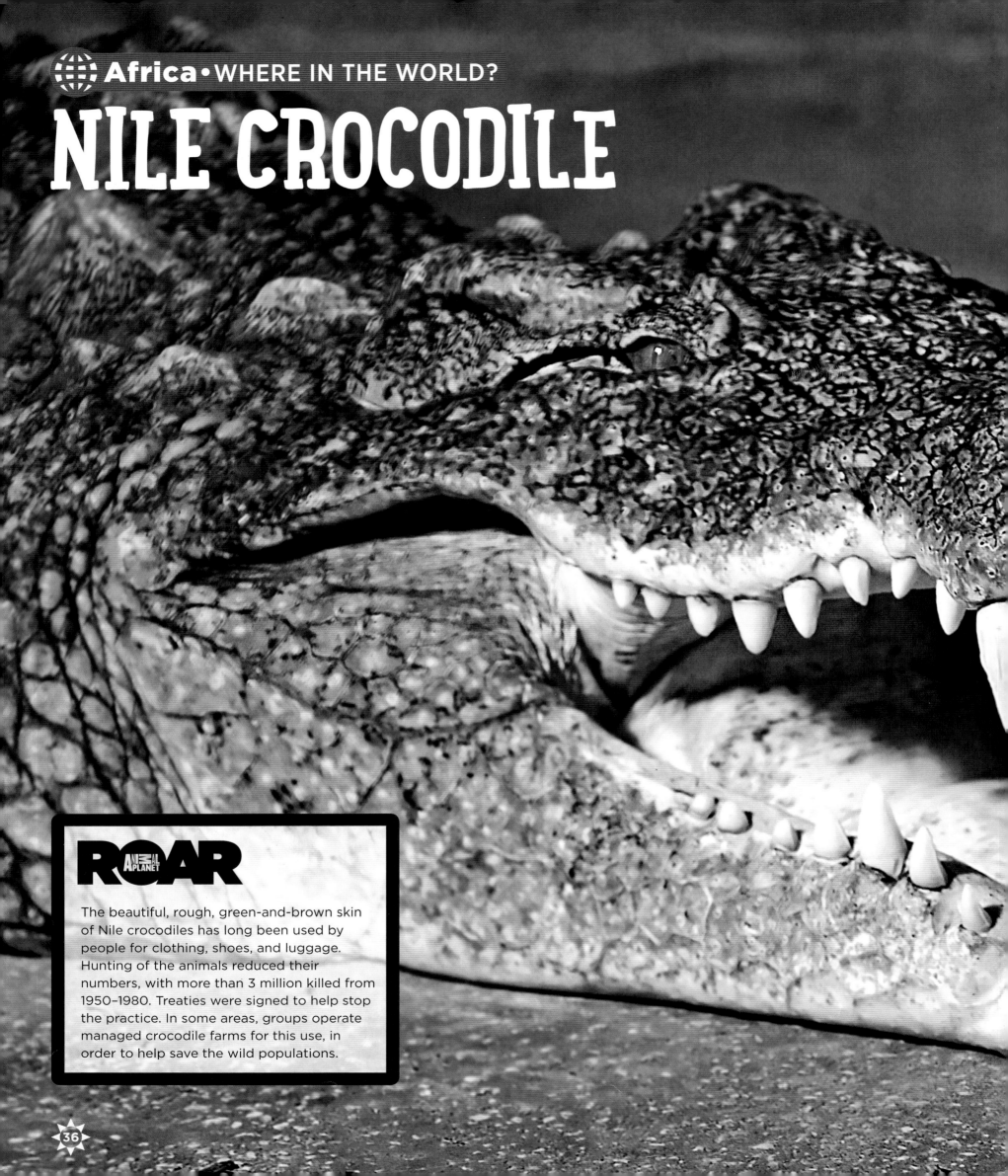

NILE CROCODILE

ROAR

The beautiful, rough, green-and-brown skin of Nile crocodiles has long been used by people for clothing, shoes, and luggage. Hunting of the animals reduced their numbers, with more than 3 million killed from 1950–1980. Treaties were signed to help stop the practice. In some areas, groups operate managed crocodile farms for this use, in order to help save the wild populations.

Animal Close Up

Crocodiles are built for life in the water. They use their long tails to swim. Their thick skin is waterproof, so they can stay in water for a long time. Their eyes and nostrils are on top of their heads, so they can float almost unseen while waiting for prey.

Animal Facts

COMMON NAME: Nile crocodile
SCIENTIFIC NAME: *Crocodylus niloticus*
LENGTH: 16-20 feet (5-6 m)
WEIGHT: 500 pounds (225 kg)
HABITAT: Swamps, marshes, rivers
DIET: Fish, mammals, reptiles

Where does it live?

Though now absent from the northern Nile itself, the Nile crocodile lives in wetlands throughout central and southeastern Africa, and on the eastern coast of Madagascar.

Why does it live there?

Crocodiles are excellent swimmers and more comfortable hunting and moving in water than on land.

What does it eat?

Crocodiles eat fish and small mammals and even birds. Nile crocodiles have been seen "herding" fish toward shore for easy prey.

Crocodiles use their mouths full of sharp teeth to latch onto prey. What happens if they break off a tooth? They grow a new one. A long-lived croc might go through 3,000 teeth in its lifetime.

⊕ EUROPE

When most people think of Europe, they picture its great cities, such as London and Paris, or famous monuments—the Roman Colosseum or Berlin's Brandenburg Gate. But even amid the bustling cities and expanding suburbs of this continent, millions of animals make their homes. Europe's biomes range from warmer forests in the south to frozen lands in the far north, with a bit of high-altitude Alpine mountains in the middle! Be a different kind of tourist on this trip to Europe—look for animals instead of historic landmarks!

ANIMAL

ANIMAL PLANET

PASSPORT

Passenger Information

NAME: **EUROPEAN TREE FROG**
SCIENTIFIC NAME: *Hyla arborea*
SIZE: 1-2.5 inches (3-5 cm)
ADDRESS: European trees
FAVORITE MEAL: Insects

— 27 —

Visas

A brownish-green stripe running down its side from each eye marks this species of amphibian. They like to hunt at night, sleeping most of the day hidden among tree leaves. Females can lay up to 1,000 eggs at a time. Like other frogs, they are born as tadpoles in water and metamorphose (change) into four-legged creatures.

— 28 —

MARINE

MARINE

TAIGA

TEMPERATE FOREST

GRASSLANDS

ALPINE

MARINE

THE EASTERN PLAINS

For most of the 20th century, Europe was split between eastern and western countries. Animals didn't care about the politics, of course. But those creatures that lived in flat grasslands found their homes mostly in the east. Spreading meadows and fields divide the forests of central Europe from the wider steppes (or grasslands) of Russia. In those fields live thousands of bird and insect species, along with the mammals and reptiles that depend on those animals for food. It's a bird-eat-bug world on Europe's grasslands.

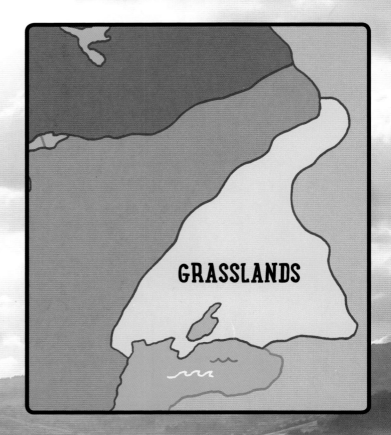

GRASSLANDS

GREAT BUSTARD

This bird is a big show-off. Male bustards display their plumage and strut around posing to attract females, who are not as decorative. They are big birds, weighing as much as 45 pounds (20 kg). They find their food in fields, which are rapidly disappearing as cities and suburbs expand. In some places, bustards have almost disappeared.

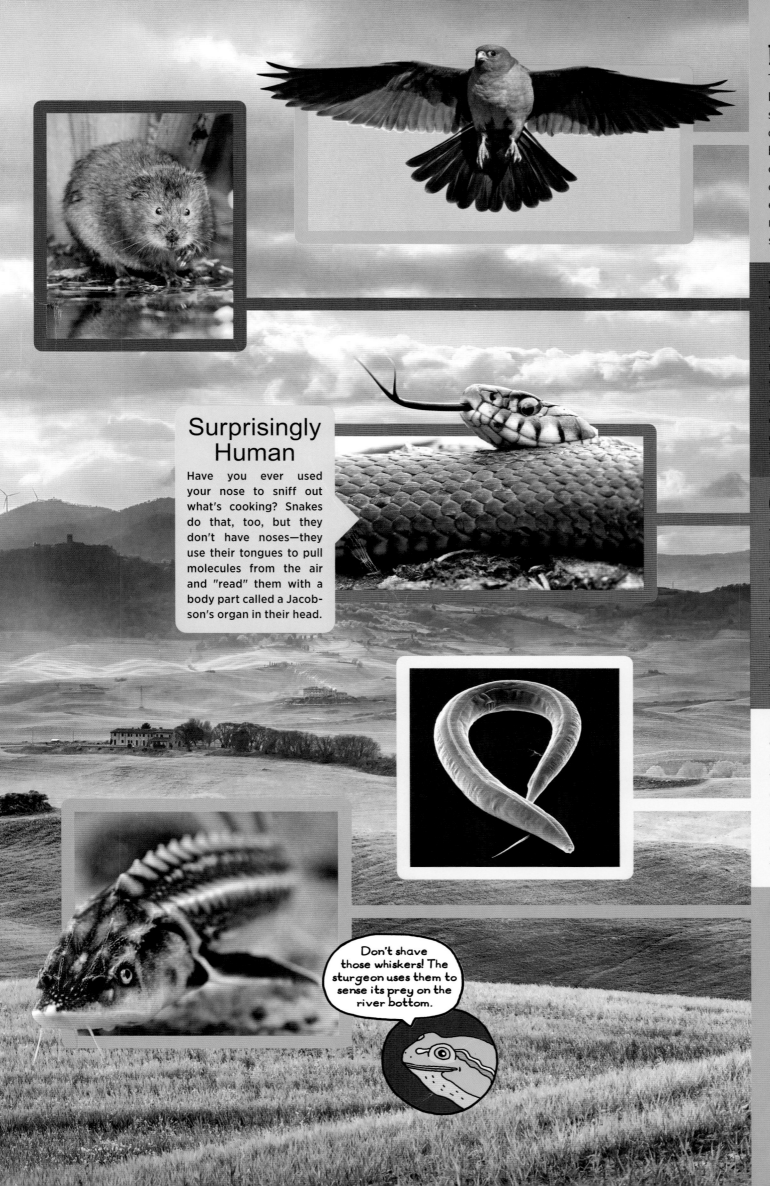

RED-FOOTED FALCON

These birds are part-time Europeans. They make summer homes and nests on the Eastern plains, but fly to warmer parts of Africa in winter. Unlike other raptors, they prefer eating insects over fish or mammals. The falcons often snag their prey in the air.

EUROPEAN WATER VOLE

Where grasslands meet water, you might find this rodent. They live in riverside burrows and eat the grasses that grow along streams and ponds. Voles can swim well, and often escape predators by taking to the water.

GRASS SNAKE

Just about every country in Europe has a grass snake species that lives mostly within its borders. About a yard long and common across the continent, they are not dangerous to people. Amphibians are their favorite prey, which they usually hunt at night.

NEMATODE

Nematodes are a family of worms. Some can be a foot (0.3 m) long, but most are much smaller. This species is 3/100 inch (1 mm) long. They eat micro-organisms, which they convert to rich soil.

RUSSIAN STURGEON

Large rivers, such as the Dnieper, Don, and Volga, run through the grasslands. They are home to this fish, the source for a highly prized food known as caviar—fish eggs. Caviar was so popular that sturgeon are endangered, but people are working to help the fish recover.

Surprisingly Human

Have you ever used your nose to sniff out what's cooking? Snakes do that, too, but they don't have noses—they use their tongues to pull molecules from the air and "read" them with a body part called a Jacob-son's organ in their head.

Don't shave those whiskers! The sturgeon uses them to sense its prey on the river bottom.

41

KESTREL

At just over a foot tall, the sharp-eyed kestrel is one of the smallest raptors. It prefers forests and meadows, but it has adapted to life in cities and towns, making nests on the sides of high buildings.

EUROPEAN BISON

At up to 11 feet (3.3 m) long and more than 2,000 pounds (907 kg), this is the largest land animal in Europe. A conservation program helped bring them back from near extinction.

NOSE-HORNED VIPER

These yard-long vipers use their fangs to inject venom into prey, usually rodents or birds. That venom usually won't kill a person, but the bite is very painful.

STAG BEETLE

This tree-loving beetle uses its long "horns" for fighting, not for gathering food. The males swing the horns like swords when they compete for mates. They are also common in gardens.

EUROPEAN TOAD

When it's time to breed and lay eggs, this toad heads to the water. The rest of the time, it waits in forests and fields for prey, such as insects, small reptiles, or spiders, to come by.

RED SQUIRREL

Nuts and seeds gathered during the fall keep this animal fed through the winter. They are being forced out of their native homes by American gray squirrels.

FADING FORESTS

Thousands of years ago, most of Europe was covered by forests. Today, most of it is covered by cities and towns—including many buildings built with the wood from those forests. However, large areas of woodland do remain from England to Spain to eastern Europe. In the shade of the forest trees, hundreds of species live on the ground, while the tree-loving birds, butterflies, and bats take to the air.

TEMPERATE FOREST

EUROPEAN BADGER

Found throughout Europe, the badger makes its home in underground dens. Powerful claws make short work of hard soil. Several badger groups work together to dig out tunnels and sleeping places. These animals are omnivores. They can catch and eat rodents and lizards, but if those aren't around, they will eat seeds, nuts, and grasses. They also eat earthworms.

When I hear one of these guys coming, I hide. Badgers like to eat (gulp!) frogs!

ALPINE SALAMANDER

One of the few amphibians that can live at high altitudes, these animals play good defense. They ooze out stinky stuff if touched, and they can play dead by displaying a "broken" neck.

ALPINE MARMOT

This member of the squirrel family survives the long alpine winter by hibernating below ground for perhaps as long as nine months. A breeding pair and their past year's young live together in multiple rooms connected by tunnels. In summer, they emerge from their tunnel homes to look for food in the meadows.

EURASIAN NUTHATCH

In their Alpine home, these birds find a place to nest and look for seeds and nuts to eat. Most birds cannot survive in the thin air at such high altitudes. They get their name from their eating behavior. To crack open, or "hatch," a nut, they wedge it into tree bark and then peck at it.

MOUNTAIN APOLLO

Rocky areas in the Alpine foothills provide stonecrop and houseleek plants, the preferred food for the caterpillars of this species of butterfly. After the caterpillars feed and grow, they make their coccons on the ground, not in plants, as many other butterflies do. One of the best places to spot the adult mountain apollo is in the beautiful and flower-filled Valais Valley in Switzerland, home to many types of butterflies.

Surprisingly Human

Who needs a handshake or a hug when you have a nose? Marmots are well-known for their cute nose-to-nose greeting behavior among family members.

Here's a cool word I learned: a person who studies butterflies is a "lepidopterist."

LIVING IN THE ALPS

The "alpine" biome gets its name from this area in southern Europe—the Alps. The highest mountain range in Europe crosses several national borders, from France to Austria. Its highest peaks are bare, but animals roam the high meadows, steep slopes, and tree-covered passes below. The biome itself stops below the tree line, the place on mountains past which trees cannot grow.

ALPINE

ALPINE IBEX

If you're afraid of heights, you'd make a terrible ibex. These large, hooved mammals spend their days on sheer cliffs and steep mountainsides looking for vegetation to eat. Their ability to climb also helps them avoid predators. Male ibex use their horns to show off for mates—or fight other males for them! Other ibex species live in the mountains in Africa and Asia.

NORTHERN REACHES

The taiga spreads out north of the temperate forest area and south of the northern tundra. The biome is a large area of forest and field that is home to dozens of hardy species. Birds migrate to warmer climates in winter, but other locals stick around and hibernate through the hard winter, or manage to find enough food to survive until spring.

TAIGA

ERMINE

The beautiful white fur of this weasel, also known as a stoat, has decorated European royal robes for centuries. The fur is only white in the winter, however, turning brown in other seasons. Ermine live in underground dens, coming out to scurry through fields looking for the small animals that make up their prey.

The enormous taiga biome, which is found in northern Europe and stretches across northern Russia and even into Canada, is under threat.

The remote terrain makes it hard to develop, but more and more places are being explored for possible oil drilling, logging, and mining. Countries are keeping an eye on this sensitive land even as moves are made to use its resources.

BARBASTELLE

Bat colonies that live in the Scandinavian taiga have a tricky job. This far north, summer days are very long. But bats usually hunt at night. These northern bats have to eat their fill of insects on short nights in summer; they then hibernate in winter.

MOUNTAIN HARE

Like many northern species, the mountain hare changes the color of its fur with the seasons. The hares shed, or "molt," their fur, changing from brown in the summer to white in the winter, the better to hide in the snow-covered taiga.

SAIIMA RINGED SEAL

This is one of the rarest animals in this book. Fewer than 400 of them exist, and they all live in Lake Saiima in southern Finland. These are one of the few freshwater seals in the world. Related to ringed seals that live in the ocean, this group must have been cut off from the sea thousands of years ago.

PUFFIN

More than 8 million of these birds live in Iceland. On an island named Haimaey, thousands live on a rock formation that looks like it would fit into another part of this book. What animal do you see?

WHOOPER SWAN

Large (with a 7-foot/2.3 m) wingspan and loud (that's where they get the name), this graceful animal is the national bird of Finland. Whooper swans pair up for life, hatching annual broods of eggs.

OLD WORLD SWALLOWTAIL

Animal Facts

COMMON NAME: Old World swallowtail butterfly
SCIENTIFIC NAME: *Papilio machaon*
WINGSPAN: 3 inches (7.5 cm)
HABITAT: Wooded areas, meadows
DIET: Nectar from flowers (adult)

Where does it live?

Swallowtails live all over the world. There are hundreds of species of swallowtails, but this one is considered the most widespread.

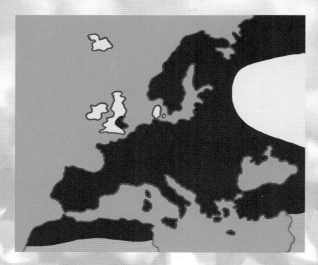

Why does it live there?

Swallowtails live anywhere that there are flowers for them to eat. That can be meadows, fields, woods, or grasslands.

What does it eat?

Swallowtail caterpillars like to eat from flowers that grow in the carrot or celery family. Adults suck nectar from flowers.

This swallowtail lives mostly on the main continent of Europe. A separate species lives in the British Isles. In 2014, however, butterfly lovers were excited to find the more common continental species living and breeding in England. While this might not seem like a big deal, the ability of a species to make a new home in a new climate and habitat can be a positive sign for the future of these butterflies.

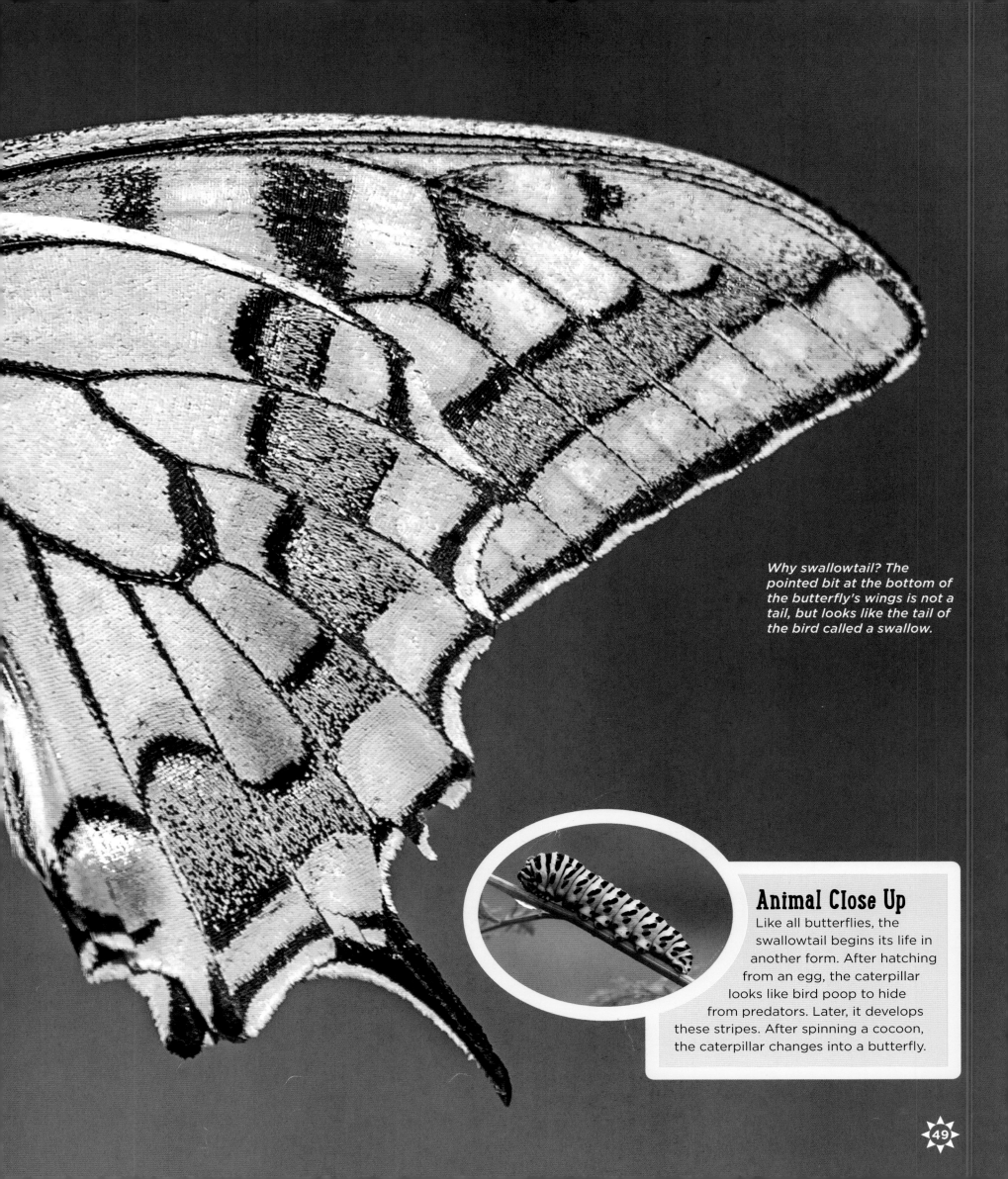

Why swallowtail? The pointed bit at the bottom of the butterfly's wings is not a tail, but looks like the tail of the bird called a swallow.

Animal Close Up

Like all butterflies, the swallowtail begins its life in another form. After hatching from an egg, the caterpillar looks like bird poop to hide from predators. Later, it develops these stripes. After spinning a cocoon, the caterpillar changes into a butterfly.

NORTH AMERICA

North America covers a lot of ground! With all that land, there is room for billions of animals (okay, millions of animals and billions of insects!). There is also room for a wide variety of biomes, stretching from the steamy rainforests of the south, through the wide-open prairies of the United States, to the frozen tundra of Canada's north. These biomes contain a wealth of familiar and unusual animals.

Passenger Information

NAME: **AMERICAN ROBIN**

SCIENTIFIC NAME: *Turdus migratorius*

SIZE: 10 inches (25.4 cm)

ADDRESS: Most of North America

FAVORITE MEAL: Worms, grubs, berries

— 27 —

Visas

Robins live in nearly every part of North America at different times of the year. They live year-round across the United States. In their summer breeding season, many fly north to Canada. When they are not breeding, they winter in warmer Mexico. Robins are well-known for their red-orange chest feathers and for being signs of spring!

— 28 —

TUNDRA

TAIGA

GRASSLANDS

TEMPERATE
FOREST

DESERT

TROPICAL
RAINFOREST

TONS OF TREES!

The temperate forest in North America includes many types of trees, from evergreens in the north and west to deciduous trees (species that drop their leaves in fall) in the central and southern parts. Most of this biome experiences all four seasons, so animals deal with all kinds of weather. Their life cycles often mirror the seasons, so look for baby animals in the spring!

TEMPERATE FOREST

WHITE-TAILED DEER
When this easily startled mammal bounds away, its tail goes up and the name is clear! Deer live at the edges of forest, near meadows and farmland. Gray in winter and brown in summer, they are a common sight in the forest. Drivers in forest areas need to be careful, since deer don't read road signs!

URBAN ANIMALS

As people and cities took over the forests, many forest animals adapted to find homes alongside humans. Peregrine falcons make their nests in tall buildings. Homes near wooded areas need tight garbage cans to keep out inventive raccoons. City or suburban parks that include many trees make good homes for gray squirrels.

NORTHERN CARDINAL

Unlike many songbirds, cardinals don't migrate. In every season, you can spot these famous red birds in the trees. The range of this popular animal is so large, seven different states have chosen it as their "official bird."

BLACK RAT SNAKE

This snake takes its name from what it often eats, not because it's fuzzy and has whiskers! They're not dangerous to humans, but don't pick them up. They spew out a very stinky, sticky goo when threatened or bothered and can bite.

GREAT PLAINS TOAD

This species likes a home near water, but spends most of its time buried in the thick vegetation of the forest floor. And yes, like many toads, it has bumps that look like warts!

PERIODICAL CICADA

The sound of summer in the eastern and midwestern U.S. includes the buzz of these insects. Some species only come out every 17 years!

Surprisingly Human

Do you wash your hands before you eat? (You should!) Raccoons need to live near water because they often need water with their food—some people say it looks like they are washing up! Since they sometimes eat garbage, not a bad idea!

Cicadas have five eyes! They have one on each side and three on top . . . I'm jealous!

GIANT DAMSELFLY

The four long wings of this rainforest insect give it the ability to hover in place, dart after prey, and fly at high speed. Its sharp feet help it snag insects out of spider webs. Some species can have wings as wide as 7 inches (7.8 cm)!

RHINOCEROS BEETLE

One guess how this insect got its name. Yup—it was named for the large horn on its head, which males use to joust with others for mates. Some species can be more than 7 inches (15.2 cm) long.

JAGUAR

A fierce predator, the jaguar takes its name from a native word for large carnivores that means "kills with one leap." The largest cat in the Americas takes care of business with sharp claws and great speed. Their spots (called rosettes) help them blend in with the shadows created on the forest floor.

PLUMED BASILISK

Wide feet and strong back legs give this reptile the ability to run (for short stretches) on top of the water. When they slow down, they can swim! Tails that can be three times as long as their bodies help them balance.

GLASS FROG

The skin of these tree-dwelling amphibians is so thin and clear, you can see their organs. That helps these shy, nocturnal creatures hide in leafy trees in the forest canopy.

This guy is thinking, "I spy with my little eyes, something starting with . . . lunch!"

A DARK GREEN REALM

Closer to the Equator, the climate turns tropical and the biome becomes a rainforest. In southern Mexico and most of Central America, large areas of thick green vegetation are filled with amazing animals. They thrive in the moist heat, whether they skitter and hop on the dark forest floor or fly and jump amid the soaring trees.

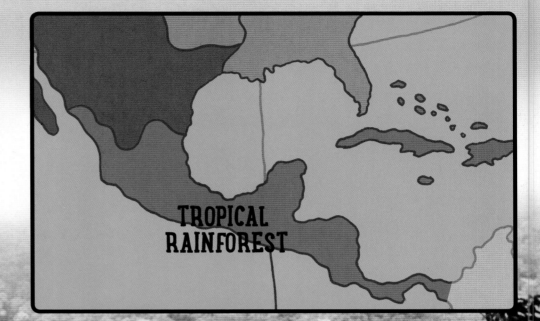

TROPICAL RAINFOREST

ROAR

Central American rainforests are some of the world's most biologically diverse areas. That means they have more species of animals and plants in their small area than some much larger biomes have. The rainforests are shrinking, however, as a result of logging, farming, and the construction of homes. The Rainforest Action Network is working to stop human activities that are harming the forest.

SCARLET MACAW

This bird, which loves to fly amid the tropical treetops, has some of the most beautiful plumage (feathers) in the world. And here's a cool fact: Most scarlet macaws use their left foot to pick up and handle their food, which is mostly fruit, while they stand or perch on their right foot.

ACROSS THE PRAIRIE

Enormous rolling miles of grasslands once covered central and western North America. Four steady seasons and wide, flat land helped the grasses grow. Over the centuries, millions of people have moved into the "Great Plains," and changed those grasslands into farms, ranches, and cities. Only a small part remains unchanged. A wide range of animals make their homes in, under, and above those wide-open spaces.

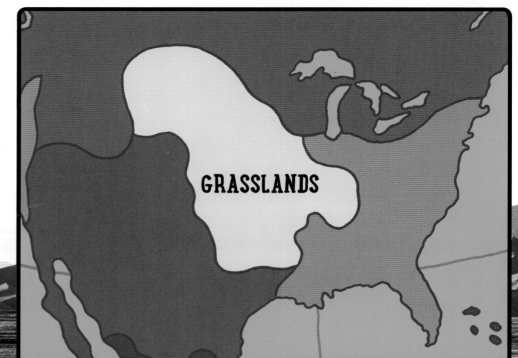

GRASSLANDS

AMERICAN BISON
Today, bison can be seen mostly in protected areas. That was not always the case. For centuries, bison dominated the Great Plains. Plains Indians reported seeing herds that stretched to the horizon. Many tribes, such as the Arapaho and the Osage, depended on these large mammals for survival. Bison also helped the wide grasslands expand. Huge herds left behind a lot of manure. That fertilized the ground to help more grass grow, and provided homes and food to insects and birds.

Surprisingly Human

Prairie dog dens have several entrances. A prairie dog stands at each like a guard, alert for trouble. Instead of using a whistle when it spots a predator such as a hawk, it squeaks to let others know to head for safety!

Adult red-tailed hawks eat rodents, snakes, and . . . uh, other birds.

PRAIRIE DOG

About a foot long, prairie dogs are rodents that live mostly in large, underground dens. The dens can have several rooms, including nurseries, storage rooms, and sleeping places. Noises they make to warn of danger led early settlers to call them "dogs."

RED-TAILED HAWK

Soaring high above the prairie on rising hot air, hawks use their amazing eyesight to seek out their favorite prey: rodents, snakes, and other birds. Pairs of hawks build their nests high atop trees or even on building ledges in urban areas.

GRASSHOPPER

Hundreds of species of this insect live in the North American grasslands. In large groups, grasshoppers can cause damage to crops and fields. Their whirring wings can be heard on quiet evenings.

WESTERN MEADOWLARK

Colorful, insect-eating meadowlarks build their nests on the ground, amid the short or tall grasses. Their song is heard throughout the grasslands.

PRAIRIE KINGSNAKE

Kingsnakes are nonvenomous hunters that usually eat rodents and other snakes. About 3 feet (0.9 m) long as adults, they are often found on farms and ranches, where their hunting skills are appreciated by human residents.

SIZZLING SANDS

Deserts in Mexico and the American Southwest feature large areas of sand, scrubby vegetation, and cactuses. Fewer plants and animals are adapted to survive in this harsh environment, but those that are can survive for months without rain, and in heat that tops 100°F (38°C) daily. The number of animals in a desert biome is smaller than in most biomes. The diversity is also not as large. But for these desert dwellers, there's no place like home.

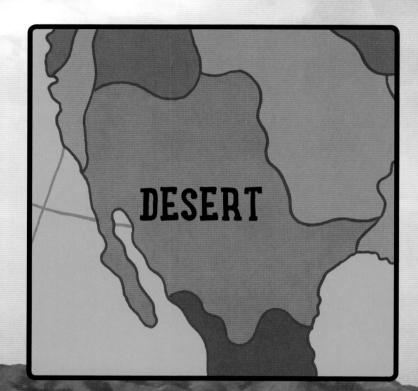

DESERT

GILA MONSTER

There are more than 6,000 species of lizards in the world. Very few of them are poisonous to people. This is one of them. Gila (HEE-lah) monsters clamp their strong jaws on prey (or bothersome people) and squeeze in venom. Like snakes, they use their forked tongue to "sniff" the air around them.

They don't say "beep beep" like in the cartoons, but they do coo and clack.

ROADRUNNER

They can fly, but they run so fast, they rarely have to. Some species can reach 35 miles per hour. Roadrunners are also quick enough to kill a rattlesnake to eat. Their speed and skills made them part of Native American legends.

JACKRABBIT

The huge ears of these zippy desert mammals have two purposes. They take in the sounds of oncoming predators, such as coyotes or hawks. And if the animal gets too hot, it can let off excess heat through its ears!

DIAMONDBACK RATTLESNAKE

The furious sound of a rattler's rattle is one of the scariest in nature. It's a warning, though, not a threat. Rattlesnakes don't want to attack people; they'd rather save their venom for prey. However, because they have to lie in the sun to absorb heat, they can find themselves in the path of people. Their bite can be deadly, so listen carefully as you hike in the desert.

HAIRY SCORPION

This arachnid gets its name from the bristles on its body that it uses to sense vibrations of oncoming prey. Its sting is painful and is used to kill prey, but is not deadly to humans.

VELVET ANT

Surprise: This is not an ant—it's a wasp. The insect's shape makes it look like an ant, however. The bristles on its back look like velvet. When bothered, it makes a raspy squeaking sound.

TREES, TREES, TREES...

Huge forests and wide meadows fill Canada's enormous taiga. While it has a harsh winter, it also enjoys a mild spring and summer. Much of the taiga has not been touched by humans, giving many animals room to thrive. Taiga animals often hibernate during those long cold months—or in the case of birds, get out of town!

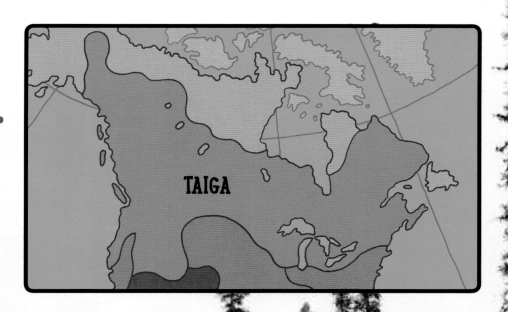

SPOTTED SALAMANDER

These small amphibians live on the forest floor near water. In fact, they spend the first part of their lives *under* water, breathing through gills. After growing, they come out on land to breathe air.

WOLVERINE

This feisty creature has evolved perfectly to survive in wintry lands, with thick fur and wide feet that won't sink in the snow. A great sense of smell helps wolverines find prey, even deep under the icy ground. Like the comic book character with the same name (and the same sharp claws!), this is one fierce creature.

YELLOW-BELLIED FLYCATCHER

Part of the taiga is covered with bogs, areas of thick, squishy ground. These birds love bogs, where they can find materials and sites for their nests, as well as insects to eat. As winter aproaches, they join a migration south, but not too far. Most stay in southern Canada.

BLACK BEAR

The Canadian taiga is not the only home for this familiar forest mammal. But the taiga is packed with things that black bears need: lots of fruit and berries (and fish) to eat; places to hibernate; and room to roam.

GREAT WHITE NORTH

Say goodbye to summer when you reach the far northern tundra region. There's not much spring or fall, either. The land in the tundra is frozen solid year-round, making survival truly only for the fittest. Tundra animals have unique adaptations that let them survive in sub-freezing conditions.

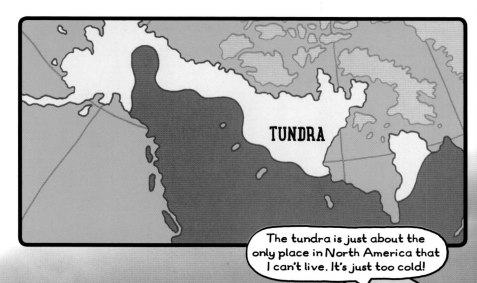

TUNDRA

The tundra is just about the only place in North America that I can't live. It's just too cold!

POLAR BEAR

Though they appear white to blend into snow and ice, polar bears actually have black skin. Their hair is transparent. When the light hits the hair, it appears white. They are top predators, but their habitat is threatened.

ARCTIC FOX

In summer, this quick and creative hunter tracks down birds and rodents. In the harsh winter months, it might find its only meal by following polar bears and looking for leftovers.

SNOWY OWL

Only a handful of birds can survive the Arctic chill. Snowy owls are the biggest; in fact, they are the heaviest owl in North America. Feathers grow over their feet to help them deal with the cold and ice. With little competition from other raptors, they hunt small rodents in the daytime (most owls hunt at night).

WALRUS

This familiar marine mammal sports some of the most famous tusks in the world. They use these large teeth to help pull their huge bodies out of the water onto ice floes, or to dig for clams in the ocean bottom. Sensitive whiskers on their face also help them feel for their underwater meals.

BALD EAGLE

ROAR

The bald eagle has been the symbol of the United States since 1782. By the early 1900s, eagle populations had dropped due to hunting and habitat destruction. Down to about 500 nesting pairs, the birds were named an endangered species in 1967. Since then, their population has grown. The conservation efforts have been so effective that this eagle has now been removed from the endangered species lists. This is one conservation success story!

Animal Facts

COMMON NAME: Bald Eagle
SCIENTIFIC NAME: *Haliaeetus leucocephalus*
WINGSPAN: 6-8 feet (3-4 m)
WEIGHT: 14 pounds (6.3 kg)
HABITAT: Wooded areas
DIET: Fish, small rodents, small birds

Where does it live?

Bald eagles live throughout North America. Most live near bodies of water such as rivers and lakes, especially with nearby wooded areas.

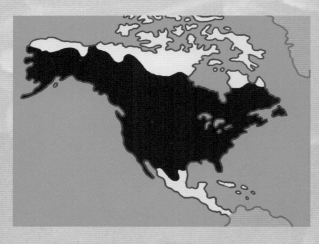

Why does it live there?

Lakes, rivers, and streams are home to the eagles' favorite food: fish. Tall trees near the water provide places for nests.

What does it eat?

Along with fish that they snatch from the water with their claws, eagles also eat rodents and larger birds such as ducks and geese.

Bald eagles make surprisingly high-pitched calls for their size and power. They have been described as sounding like a flute.

Animal Close Up

Bald eagles are not bald, of course. They don't have any hair at all! The white feathers of adult males gave the bird its famous name. Younger eagles have brown head feathers that become white as the animal ages.

⊕ SOUTH AMERICA

When most people think of South America, they think of one thing—the Amazon River rainforest. Indeed, that animal home in South America is nearly as large as the United States (without Alaska and Hawaii). Its amazing biodiversity makes this continent worth looking at all by itself. But there's more to South America than just a rainforest. Wide grasslands cover some southern areas, while the driest deserts in the world line the southwestern coast. In the west, the mighty Andes mountains rise into the clouds. South America is a busy place!

ANIMAL ANIMAL PLANET PASSPORT

Passenger Information

NAME: **MARINE IGUANA**
SCIENTIFIC NAME: *Amblyrhynchus cristatus*
SIZE: 3 feet (0.9 m)
ADDRESS: Galapagos Islands
FAVORITE MEAL: Algae, seaweed
— 27 —

Visas

See those little orange specks to the west (left) of South America? Those are the Galapagos Islands, home to one of the only lizards that dives and feeds in the ocean. Marine iguanas eat algae that grows on underwater rocks. They can spend up to 30 minutes underwater, but have to come back to shore to warm up.
— 28 —

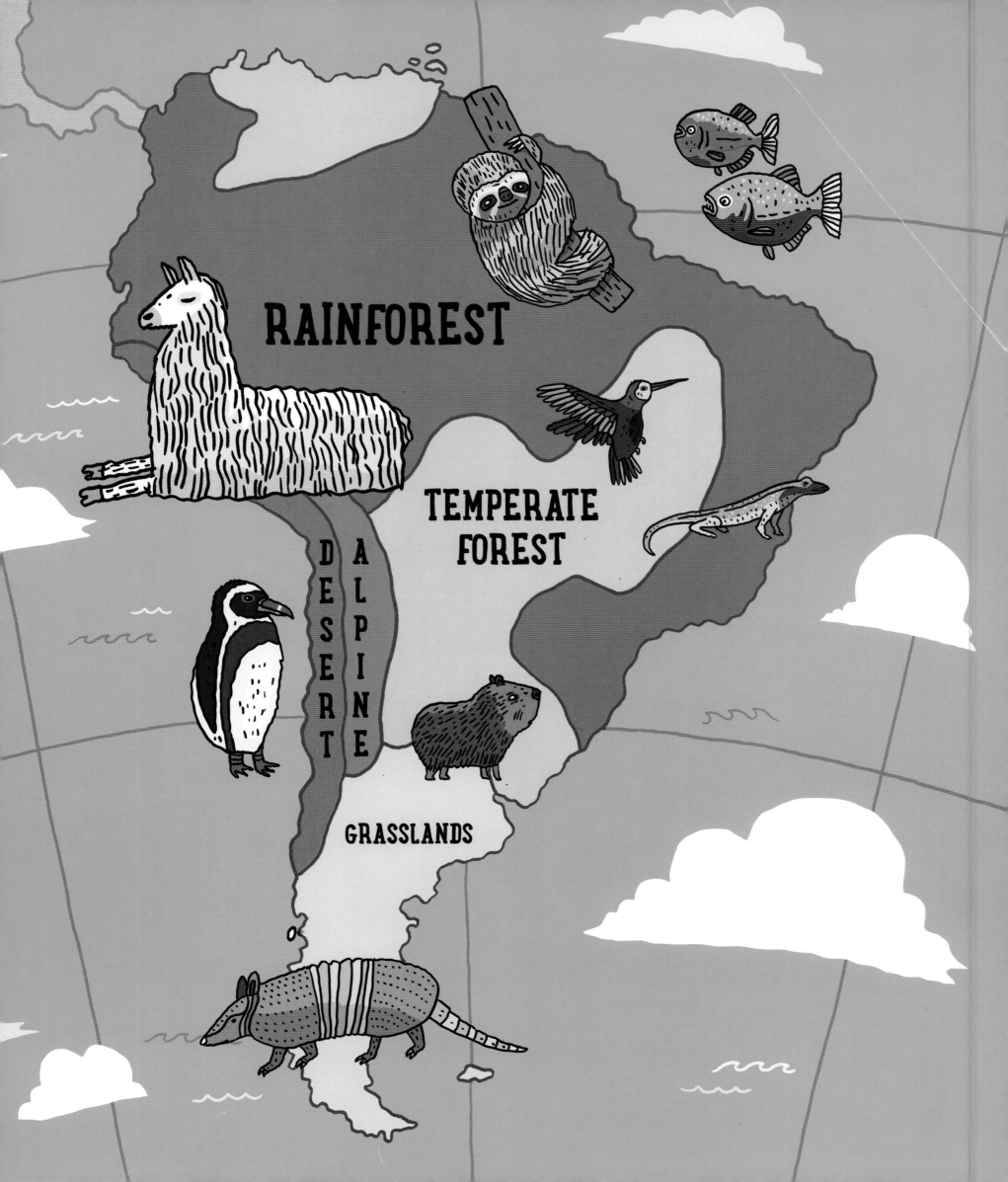

RAINFOREST

TEMPERATE FOREST

DESERT ALPINE

GRASSLANDS

GIANT RIVER OTTER

This is the largest otter species in the world. They hunt for fish, crabs, and snakes in rivers and lakes. Those long whiskers do more than look good—they are used like antennae to help the animals locate underwater prey.

PYGMY ROUND-EARED BAT

Those big ears hear echoes of the squeaking sounds the bats make as they fly. That helps this species locate insects to eat. These bats often live near rivers or streams.

TAPIR

Scientists think that tapirs are one of the animals that has changed the least over millions of years. Fossil tapirs look almost exactly like modern ones. Tapirs eat fruits and plants, but they also love to be in the water, where they cool off and eat water vegetation. Their poop is a key way that many seeds are spread.

SQUIRREL MONKEY

Even though its tail is usually longer than its 10-inch (25 cm) body, this monkey can't use it to grab. The tail does come in handy for balance in the trees. These very intelligent animals live together in troops of dozens of individuals.

TOUCAN

The toucan is famous for its long, colorful beak, which is sometimes as big as its whole body! It uses the beak's sharp edges to grab and crush fruit or to reach into holes in trees.

What a nose! It can be a snorkel when they swim or an extra hand for grabbing fruit or leaves!

AMAZING AMAZON

Hot, wet, green, dense, and mysterious: the enormous rainforest around the Amazon River basin is home to one of the most diverse groups of animals and plants in the world. Their habitats range from the thick, dark soil on the ground, to the vines and creepers that crawl up tall trees, to the very tops of those trees. In the waters of the river, creatures of many kinds swim, live, and eat. The rainforest covers parts of every South American country but the four in the south.

RAINFOREST

Surprisingly Human

Do you go to the bathroom in the same room you eat and sleep in? No, right? Neither do sloths. They live their entire lives in trees, but about once a week, they climb down to the ground to poop!

THREE-TOED SLOTH

Few animals move as slowly as a sloth. They climb slowly, eat slowly, and even digest their food slowly. That food is all plants that they find on and around their home in the trees. Those sharp claws help them hang onto branches or cut fruit or leaves. Sloths often have green algae growing on their fur, which helps them hide in trees.

I thought I was pretty big, but these snakes can be more than six feet (2 m) long!

EMERALD TREE BOA

These long snakes spend most of their lives in the trees of the rainforest. Coiled around a branch and camouflaged in green, they lie in wait for prey such as rodents, lizards, and even birds. Dangling from a branch, they can sometimes snag birds in flight. After squeezing their prey, they swallow it whole.

ROAR
ANIMAL PLANET

The Amazon rainforest is home to a third of the animal species in the world and a quarter of the fresh water. Its trees pump out oxygen we need to live. But it is disappearing. Each year, millions of acres are cut down or burned for farmland or logging. Roads are being cut to reach new logging sites. And climate change is making it hard to grow new forest. Saving the rainforest will be a big job!

BLACK CAIMAN
This relative of the alligator can reach 17 feet (5.2m) long. They feed mostly on fish and amphibians, but can take small mammals on land or from the sides of the river.

GOLIATH BIRD-EATING SPIDER
One of the many species of tarantula living in the rainforest, this enormous spider can grow to be 11 inches (28 cm) across. It's one of the world's largest.

AMAZON WOOD LIZARD
This bright-throated lizard lives in the western Amazon rainforest. To hide from predators, it lies along a branch; its brown and green skin makes it look like part of the wood. It is a diurnal hunter, which means it looks for its prey, insects, in daytime.

BUTTERFLIES
Amid the green world of the Amazon, tens of thousands of butterflies flit about. Some have amazing colors, such as the blue morpho (top left) while this clearwing (right) uses camouflage to "disappear." More than a thousand species of metalmark butterflies are native to the forests. Many have "eye" spots on their wings to fool predators (bottom left).

PIRANHA
Piranhas are small but fierce, with many sharp teeth. They often feed together in a large group, usually on fish. However, the idea that they can devour a whole cow in seconds is a myth!

GILDED HUMMINGBIRD

The colors of these tiny birds are almost as bright as the flowers from which they sip nectar. Hummingbirds work and live alone, except for when the parents are tending to eggs.

CHILEAN MOUNTAIN FALSE TOAD

It's called a false toad because at first it was thought to be one, but it's really a frog. It's also very endangered. It was first seen in 1899 and then not again for 100 years!

LION TAMARIN

Four different species of these golden-haired monkeys live in Brazilian forests, but there are not many left. Fewer than 4,000 are known to exist. Their home forests have been reduced dramatically as people build more and more cities. The few animals that remain look for insects and fruit in the trees.

MAGELLANIC WOODPECKER

These birds actually live in a small temperate forest on the southwestern tip of the continent. Only the males have those red head feathers. These birds peck into wood to find larvae.

MONITO DEL MONTE

This cute little animal is related to the opossum. Like those North American animals, it is a marsupial and carries its young in a small pouch. Monitos mostly eat invertebrates.

Surprisingly Human

Next time you use a straw, imagine you're a hummingbird. To reach the nectar they eat, these birds poke their long bills into flowers and then slurp out their long, thin tongues to lap up the juice.

Why lion? Take a look at that mane of golden hair and you'll have your answer!

WARM—NOT AS WET

To the north and south of the Amazon rainforest are other large areas of forestland. Some areas are wet enough to be called temperate rainforests, drier areas where the temperatures can be cooler are temperate forests. The less-rainy areas, which are also home to several large cities in Brazil and Venezuela, include ripe areas for animal life, with rolling hills and open meadows amid stands of trees.

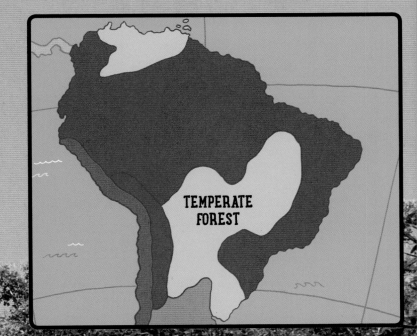

TEMPERATE FOREST

NORTHERN PUDU

In the forests of southern Brazil and northern Argentina, and in some mountain areas to the west, lives the world's smallest deer. The pudu grows to be only about a foot (30.1 cm) tall at the shoulder. When you're that small, you find new ways to escape predators such as cougars and foxes. Pudu are so nimble they can scamper onto low-hanging branches and into trees.

LIFE ON THE PAMPAS

North America has the prairie; Africa has the savanna; South America has—the *pampas*. The pampas are mostly flat, with huge open areas of grasses and scrubland. Some parts are drier than others, but the land includes only a few rolling hills. The wild pampas, mostly in Argentina and Chile, are getting smaller. Cowboys known as *gauchos* raise cattle on some parts. Huge farms grow crops like corn and wheat to support the nations' people. Vineyards grow grapes to make wine, but preserves have kept some pampas lands wild and natural.

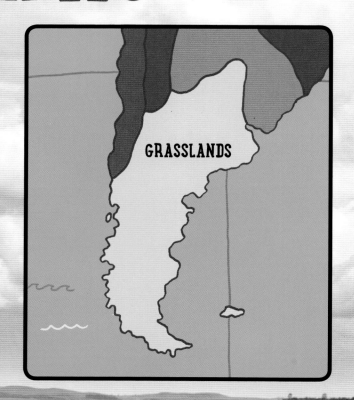

GRASSLANDS

NAKED-TAILED ARMADILLO

This armadillo lives in burrows beneath the grasslands. It eats insects, using its sharp claws to dig into their nests. Like a knight of old, the armadillo carries armor on its back. If its hard outer shell isn't enough protection from a predator, it can bury itself in the ground in a very short time.

GEOFFROY'S CAT

This feline looks a little like a household pet—it's even about the same size. But don't be fooled. This is one of the world's smallest wild cats. It survives on the pampas by doing what cats do best—chasing mice! Sadly, it is also often hunted for its beautiful fur.

GREATER RHEA

It's not a surprise that this tall, flightless bird—the largest in South America—is related to the ostrich. Like those African birds, the rhea can run very fast and can use its strong legs to kick in defense. It will eat just about anything from fruit and seeds to insects, frogs, and mice.

WOOD STORK

In the wetlands that occur in the northern part of the pampas, these wading birds find fish to eat. Their long legs stalk through the shallows, while their sharp, pointed beaks are used to snag prey. These birds often migrate to Florida during breeding season.

CAPYBARA

The capybara's scientific name comes from the Latin for "water hog." Though it looks a little pig-like, this is actually the world's largest rodent. It eats plants, chopping stalks with its sharp front teeth.

Don't fall for this trick: Maned wolves will sometime tap their feet on the ground to fool prey into coming out to see who it is!

MANED WOLF

It's called a wolf, but it is more closely related to the fox. It can turn its ears like radar dishes to seek out the sounds of prey. It mainly eats fruit, but hunts for rabbits, rodents, and fish.

73

THE DESOLATE COAST

The west coast of South America includes the Atacama Desert, one of the driest spots on the Earth. South America also has desert areas in the northeast, dryer grassland areas in the northeast, and a small, dry region on the southern tip of the continent (not shown). In these harsh lands, only the toughest animals flourish.

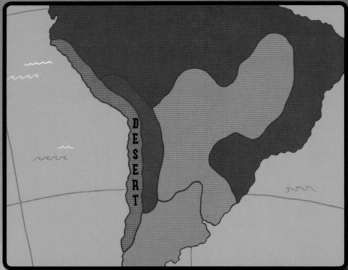

SOUTHERN VISCACHA

These long-tailed rodents live on the rocky and hilly areas on the edges of the southwestern deserts. Those big ears help them hear approaching predators. When threatened, viscachas make barking sounds and scamper back into their rocky homes.

BLACK-HEADED LIZARD

Lizards thrive in the desert. Like most reptiles, they need the sun to keep their bodies warm. The hot, dry air (most of the year) in the Atacama gives this lizard plenty of basking time. It lives among the rocks when it's not searching for insects to eat.

> These penguins sometimes make their nests in guano (hardened bird poop)!

CHILEAN FLAMINGO

Parts of the Atacama Desert get less than a tenth of an inch (.25 cm) of rain a year. But enough rain falls and collects on huge salt flats, called "salars," to attract these famous pink birds. They don't start out pink, but their feathers change color as they eat shrimp. Flamingoes gather in huge flocks in ponds on the salt flats, adding a splash of color to a bleak and forbidding landscape.

HUMBOLDT PENGUIN

Penguins in the desert? Almost! These small birds live on the coast where the desert reaches the sea. They are one of several penguin species living on the continent. They were named for famous German naturalist Alexander von Humboldt.

HIGH IN THE ANDES

The highest points in South America—and the coldest—are found in the Andes Mountains. It is the longest mountain range in the world and second highest after Asia's Himalayas. But on the Andes' snowy peaks or nearby foothills live a mix of interesting animals. People, too, have made their homes here, most notably the ancient Inca civilization.

O'SHAUGHNESSY'S ANOLE

The Andes include a region of "cloud forest," a high-altitude tropical area. The climate is perfect for lizards, including this insect-eating anole. It springs from leaf to leaf in search of prey.

MOUNTAIN FROG

The foothills and cloud forests of the lower Andes are home to hundreds of species of insect-loving frogs. This one, which doesn't really have a common name (its scientific name is *Bryophryne nubilosus*), can survive at altitudes of nearly 10,000 feet (3,048 m).

LLAMA

Perhaps the most well-known Andes animal is this large relative of the camel. The llama's steady footing and its ability to breathe at high altitudes have made it a valuable companion and worker for centuries. Its wool is also used to make warm clothing for locals. Along with being strong, it is known for its ability to spit!

ANDEAN CONDOR

With a wingspan of more than 10 feet (3 m), this is one of the largest flying birds in the world. Those wings come in handy when cruising on the wind. These raptors, which feed mostly on carrion (dead animals), have been spotted flying at more than 18,000 feet (5,486 m) in the air.

ANACONDA

Animal Facts

COMMON NAME: Green anaconda
SCIENTIFIC NAME: *Eunectes murinus*
LENGTH: 25-30 feet (7.6-9.1 m)
WEIGHT: 500 pounds (227 kg)
HABITAT: Rainforest, rivers
DIET: Animals of all kinds

Where does it live?

Anacondas live in or near rivers and streams throughout the Amazon River basin and rainforest.

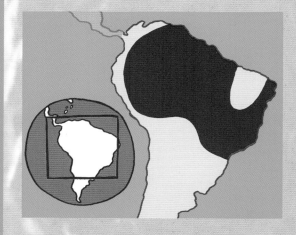

Why does it live there?

These snakes are so heavy, they can't move well on land, but they can swim well. The waterway becomes a highway.

What does it eat?

Anything it can catch, from fish and other snakes, to small mammals like pigs, to very large mammals such as deer or crocodiles.

Animal Close Up

It takes many strong people to move an anaconda around. These handlers also have to watch out for the snake's sharp fangs. The fangs will not deliver dangerous venom, but they can give a very painful bite.

Anacondas are a type of constrictor snake. After grabbing and killing prey by surrounding it with powerful, coiled muscles, the snake can unhinge its jaws to swallow animals of just about any size . . . whole!

MARINE

DESERT

TEMPERATE
FOREST

SAVANNA

MARINE

AUSTRALIA

Is Australia an island? A continent? Or is it both?! It's certainly a continent, but geographers disagree about whether it counts as an island, too. Whatever you call it, Australia is nearly as big as the continental United States, but has less than 10 percent of America's population. Its remote location means that some of the most unusual animals in the world have evolved here. There are thousands of species that can be found only in the "land down under."

MARINE

ANIMAL
ANIMAL
PLANET
PASSPO

Passenger Information

NAME: TASMANIAN DEVIL

SCIENTIFIC NAME: *Sarcophilus harrisii*
HEIGHT: 30 inches (76 cm)
ADDRESS: Tasmania (island)
FAVORITE MEAL: Small mammals, reptiles, carcasses.

— 27 —

Visas

Few animals are as fierce and ill-tempered as this marsupial. They fear almost nothing and will eat almost anything. Their screeching cries echo through the nighttime forest. Sadly, Tasmanian devils are threatened by a disease that has killed more than 90 percent of some populations. Fight on, devils!

— 28 —

INTO THE OUTBACK

Formidable deserts and dry grasslands, called savanna, cover most of the central and western part of Australia. Most of the human population lives along the coast of the continent. There are areas of trees, marshes, and grasslands, but most of the land is a red dirt area Aussies call "the Outback." To the east is an area of savanna that gets more rain and is home to other animals.

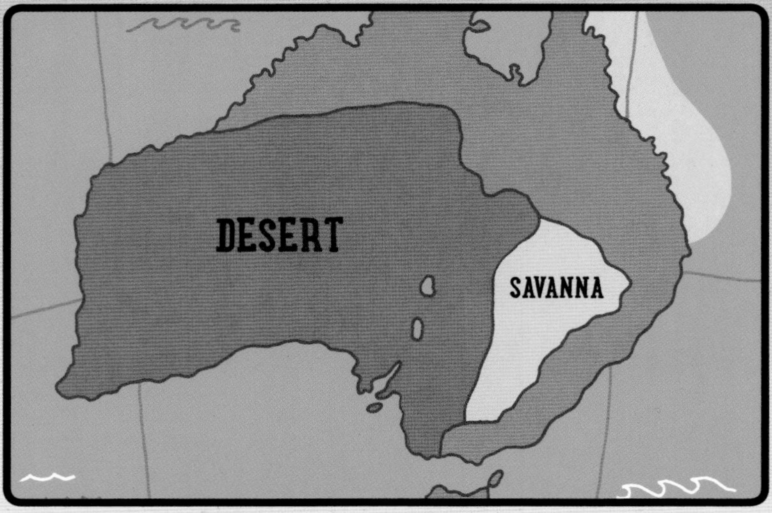

DESERT

SAVANNA

KOOKABURRA

These birds—part of the kingfisher family—live in forested areas at the edges of the Outback. Pictured here is the blue-winged species, one of four that live in Australia. They eat insects and small fish, but also can kill snakes to eat.

If emus played basketball, they could dunk. They can jump more than 7 feet (2.1 m) in the air!

EMU

At home in the savanna east of the Outback, emus depend on long, strong legs to get around. These giant birds can't fly, but can run almost as fast as an ostrich (about 40 mph!). Emus can grow up to 6 feet (2 m) tall, weigh as much as 120 pounds (54 kg), and lay eggs that are ten times larger than chicken eggs!

BARKING SPIDER

This tarantula takes its name from the raspy sounds it makes by rubbing its sharp leg bristles against pointed spines on its jaw. These spiders live underground, digging burrows in the sand. There they wait at the entrance for prey to come by—then they strike! More than 6 inches (15 cm) across, they can even capture small birds!

DINGO

These wild dogs are Australia's largest carnivorous mammal. Dingos hunt in packs, but they also stake out territory that they will strongly defend. Their main prey is small mammals, but they will attack farm animals when pickings are slim elsewhere.

GREAT GROWING WEATHER

Australia's eastern coast gets more rain than the dusty Outback, so forests flourish there. Most areas are temperate, but some are hot and wet enough to be called tropical rainforests. Several major cities are on the East Coast and have cut into this habitat, but animals still have plenty of room to roam and trees to climb.

TEMPERATE FOREST

SOUTHERN FOREST DRAGON

A patient hunter in the wetter areas of the forest, this reptile uses camouflage to hide amid branches and leaves. When an insect, smaller reptile, or spider comes by, it springs out for the kill.

WOMBAT

These cuddly-looking marsupials live in burrows they create using wide, strong paws with sharp claws. A wombat mother's pouch—home to its young, known as a joey—faces backward so it doesn't fill with dirt when digging. For defense, they turn tail— their bottom sports a tough plate of skin!

YELLOW-TAILED BLACK COCKATOO

Along with their tail feathers, these birds have face patches that are yellow. They're good parents. While mom guards the egg, dad brings home food.

KOALA

Behind the kangaroo, koalas are probably Australia's most famous animal. Fuzzy, cute, and nearly always sleeping (up to 20 hours a day!), koalas live in the eucalyptus trees that make up their entire diet. Like kangaroos, they are marsupials. Baby koalas are about the size of a jellybean!

THE AMAZING REEF

Australia is surrounded by water, of course, which is home to millions of animals. Along its northeastern coast, however, is one of the most amazing animal homes anywhere—the Great Barrier Reef. At more than 1,500 miles (2,414 km) long, it would stretch from Los Angeles to Chicago. Miles and miles of living coral, tiny islands, and sandy beaches are home to nearly 2,000 types of fish and more than 600 species of coral and other sea creatures. It's one of the most popular places to visit, and people in Australia are working hard to protect this natural wonder.

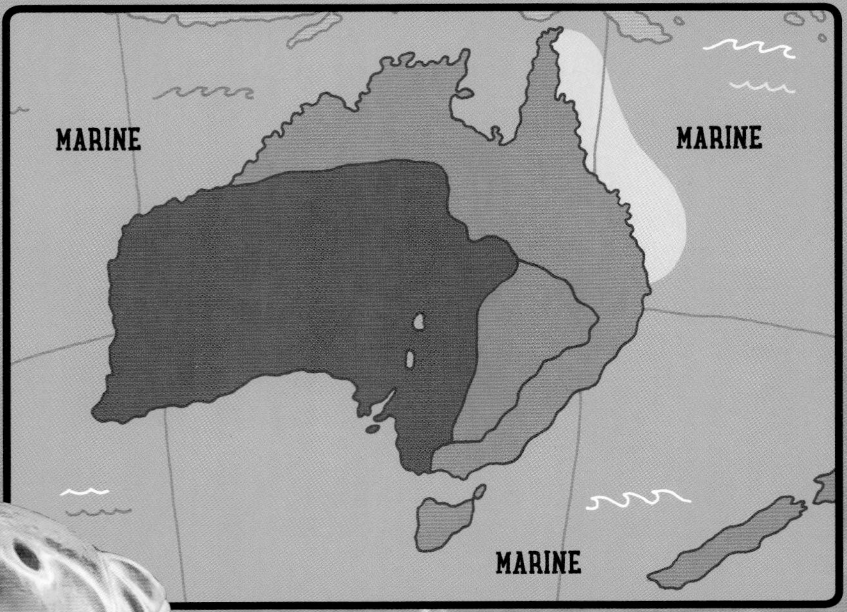

MARINE

MARINE

MARINE

GREEN SEA TURTLE

Tens of thousands of green sea turtles return each year to tiny islands along the Great Barrier Reef to lay their eggs. The animals are threatened by fishing as well as by plastic in the ocean. They confuse plastic bags with jellyfish, their favorite food.

World climate change is making the water of the reef more acidic, which is very bad for animals. Reducing the carbon dioxide we put into the air will greatly help the reef and the ocean!

SALTWATER CROCODILE

Averaging 1,000 pounds (450 kg), these are Earth's largest reptiles. Great swimmers and fierce hunters, they can live in any type of water. They eat any animal they can grab, even cows and, on occasion, people.

GIANT CLAM

Living more than 100 years and weighing as much as 450 pounds (204 kg), this is one big mollusk! Giant clams are filter feeders. They take seawater into their bodies, strain out tiny animals to eat, and release the water. Algae growing on the clams can give them bright colors.

WHALE SHARK

This is a whale of a fish. At more than 30 feet (9.1 m) long and weighing more than 20,000 pounds (9,070 kg), it's the largest fish in the world. Whale sharks are no threat to people, though. Their huge mouths filter tiny animals out of the water.

REEF FISH

The tropical fish on the Reef come in an amazing variety of shapes and colors. More than 1,500 species of mostly small fish live among the coral. Clockwise from top left: The Moorish idol features yellow-and-black stripes. The emperor angelfish is a vibrant blue. The beaked coralfish, which pokes its tiny snout into coral crevices to feed, glows orange. The foxface gets its name from the shape of its snout. Scientists think their displays of color help fish attract mates by standing out amid the duller-colored corals.

KANGAROO

Animal Close Up

The powerful hind legs of the kangaroo create its familiar hopping motion. They can spring along at 40 miles (64 kg) per hour for short stretches while making leaps that can be as long as 25 feet (7.6 m). Those legs can also be used as weapons by battling males.

Animal Facts

COMMON NAME: Red kangaroo

SCIENTIFIC NAME: *Macropus rufus*

HEIGHT: 4-5 feet (1.2–1.5 m)

WEIGHT: 200 pounds (90 kg)

HABITAT: Savannas and woodlands

DIET: Plants of all sorts

Where does it live?

Red kangaroos are found nearly all across Australia, from the harsh Outback to the wetter woodlands of the east.

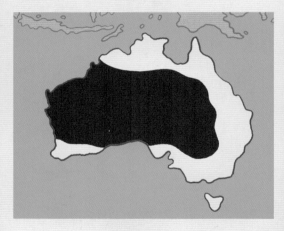

Why does it live there?

'Roos need room to roam to find their food. Wide-open spaces provide grazing land.

What does it eat?

As herbivores, kangaroos eat plants. Like cows, they re-chew their food as cud, using a multi-part stomach to digest grasses that other animals might not be able to eat.

This is a red kangaroo. Two species of grey kangaroo are smaller and live in a less widespread area.

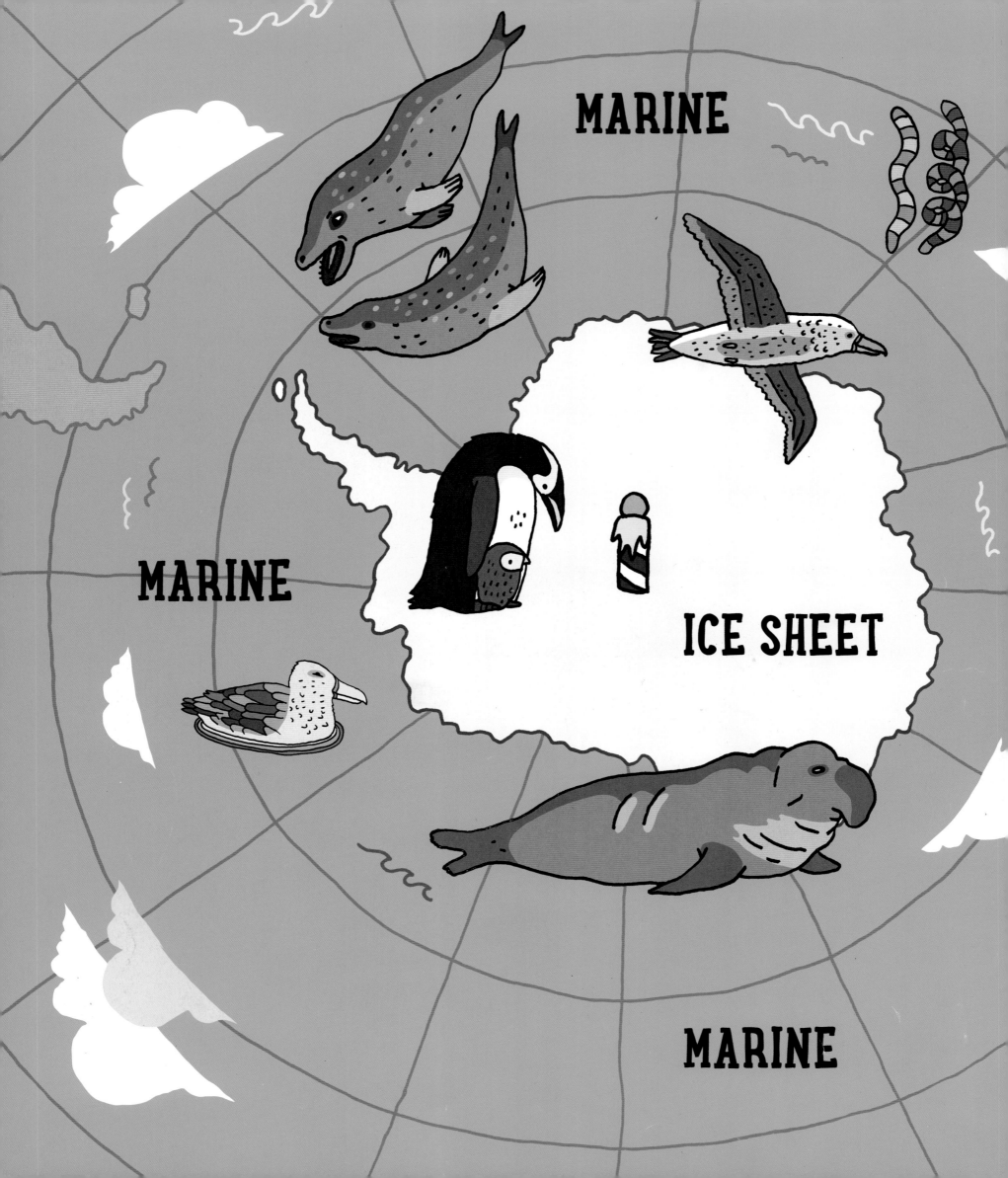

ANTARCTICA

The coldest, most remote, and emptiest continent is at the bottom of the Earth, centered on the South Pole. Even in a place where the temperature only rarely goes above freezing, and where almost nothing grows, animals find a way to survive. All the animals live on the edges of the enormous ice sheet that covers the landmass of Antarctica. That puts them in or very near the ocean, which is where they find their food.

88 MARINE
Survival of the Chilliest

89 ICE SHEET
Life on the Edge of the Ice

ANIMAL PLANET PASSPORT

Passenger Information

NAME: **CHINSTRAP PENGUIN**
SCIENTIFIC NAME: *Pygoscelis antarctica*
HEIGHT: 28 inches (70 cm)
ADDRESS: Islands near Antarctica
FAVORITE MEAL: Krill and small fish.

— 27 —

Visas

That's not a cap on the penguin's head . . . it's a line of black feathers that looks like a strap holding on a hat. This penguin dines on krill, which are tiny crustaceans that thrive in cold waters. It only rarely lives on Antarctica itself, but makes its home in huge colonies on the small islands off the continent's coast, including South Georgia and the Shetlands.

— 28 —

SURVIVAL OF THE CHILLIEST

The water surrounding Antarctica hovers between 28 and 32 degrees F (–2 to 0 C). Saltwater has a lower freezing temperature than freshwater. Water that cold would kill many animals, but millions of sea creatures (and marine mammals) live here. These include microscopic zooplankton as well as dozens of species of fish.

ROAR ANIMAL PLANET

No single country "owns" Antarctica. It is shared by many through an international treaty. This document guides scientific research while protecting the environment from waste from ships, mining, or building structures. It even bans sled dogs out of fears they would spread disease to local seal populations.

DRAGONFISH

Several species of these fish live on the bottom of the sea in Antarctica. They use their long, flat snouts to dig for small fish, tiny crustaceans, and shrimp. Unlike many fish, dragonfish eggs grow for many months before they are ready to hatch.

RIBBON WORMS

These are the long, skinny, worms in the picture (mixed with sea stars). Their squishy bodies help them survive in the cold and pressure of Antarctic seas. They swarm over fish carcasses to eat.

Yes, those teeth hurt. When we see one of these guys nearby, we get away . . . fast!

LEOPARD SEAL

Sharp-toothed leopard seals get their names from the spots on their fur, but they are also fierce hunters like their namesake. They prey on penguins, seabirds, and fish. Powerful swimmers and about 10 feet (1.6 m) long, they can also leap onto the ice to nab prey.

LIFE ON THE EDGE OF THE ICE

The thick ice sheet that covers Antarctica does not offer shelter for animals, but it is a safe refuge from the sea. Some seabirds make nests on rocky shores or cliffs. Sea mammals spend most of their time in the ocean feeding. Then they haul out on ice sheets for a safe place to give birth and rest.

Fishermen consider albatrosses to be good luck! When a seaman sees one of the birds, he knows land is probably near.

ALBATROSS

This bird's wingspan of 11 feet (3.3 m) is the largest in the world. It uses those huge wings to float for many miles above empty ocean, keeping an eye out for fish to catch.

ANTARCTIC MIDGE

The only insect native to Antarctica is a flightless fly and the largest land animal on the continent! It spends nearly all of its life as a larva, eating algae, then becomes an adult for only about a week to mate and then die.

SOUTHERN ELEPHANT SEAL

These huge mammals can weigh as much as 6,000 pounds (2,721 kg)! They may look like lumpy blobs on land, but they are excellent swimmers. Elephant seals dive nearly a mile deep and stay underwater for more than an hour. Their giant, flappy noses give them their name.

EMPEROR PENGUIN

At more than three feet (1 m) tall, these are the largest species of penguin. After each laying an egg, the female penguins return to the sea to eat. The male penguins remain behind, standing in the cold and wind while holding their eggs on their feet to keep it from freezing on the ice.

AMERICAS TO AFRICA

Oceans cover 70 percent of the Earth's surface, so the marine biome is the world's largest. Millions of animals live there, near the sunny surface, in shallow coastal waters, and in the inky-black depths. Sea creatures' homes vary in temperature, depth, and salinity (how salty the water is). Scientists divide the ocean into "zones" based on how deep the water is. Most sea animals have adapted to survive best in a particular zone.

ATLANTIC OCEAN

PURPLE-STRIPED JELLYFISH

The gooey bodies of these creatures are only a few inches across, but their tentacles extend for many feet. They use those stinging strings to trap prey, including fish and plankton. The sting of some jellies can be deadly to humans, too. Like all jellies, the warm-water-loving purple-stripes don't have lungs or gills, instead they take oxygen from the water through their skin.

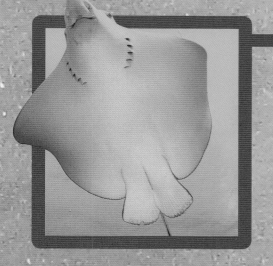

EAGLE RAY

Smooth-swimming eagle rays are light on the bottom, making it difficult for animals to see them when looking up from below, and darker on the top. They move like a bird underwater, flapping wide fins like wings. Eagle rays like warmer, shallow water, so they live near coasts at the Equator.

AMERICAN LOBSTER

This 2-foot (61 cm) long Atlantic crustacean has large front claws, antennae, ten legs, and a hard outer shell. On the ocean bottom, the lobster finds food—live and dead fish, clams, and mussels—by "tasting" using organs located on its legs.

Surprisingly Human

Human beings stay inside their mothers for nine months before being born. Lobster eggs remain inside a mother lobster for about nine months (though sometimes a bit longer) before hatching.

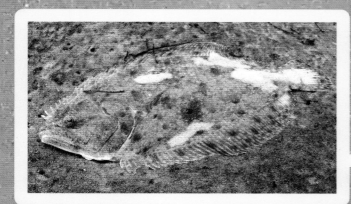

FLOUNDER

Can you spot this flat fish hiding on the bottom? The flounder is one of many sea creatures that use camouflage to hide from predators (or prey). When grown, the flounder has both eyes on the side of its body that faces up as it lies down.

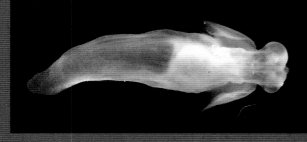

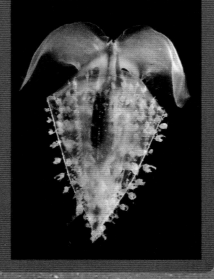

ZOOPLANKTON

The world's oceans are home to billions of animals called zooplankton, many of which are so small that you need a microscope to see them. These animals float throughout the ocean's waters at various depths. They are a key food source for thousands of other, larger species. Zooplankton include shrimp-like amphipods (top left); krill (top right), a key part of many whales' diet; sea angels (bottom left); and sea butterflies (bottom right), which are related to sea snails and sea slugs.

SUNFISH

Eight feet (2.4 m) long and weighing more than 2,000 pounds (907 kg), a sunfish can dwarf a diver. It gets its name from the habit of basking in surface sunlight before diving deep to eat jellyfish.

THORNY SEAHORSE

These six-inch (15 cm) animals get their name from the shape of their head, of course. They move using tiny fins but can cling to sea grasses with their flexible tails. For food, they look for tiny zooplankton or small crustaceans.

CLOWNFISH

Pacific islands often have coral reefs, home to millions of tropical fish such as this one. There's also another animal in this photo. The tentacles of this anemone are poisonous to other fish, but provide a safe hiding place for clownfish.

OCTOPUS

Octopuses are large-headed, blobby creatures with eight arms. The suckers on their arms help them move across rocks on coastal bottoms and grab prey such as fish or crabs.

ULTRA-DEEP LIFE

These fish are adapted to life in the deepest Pacific, 30,000 feet (9,144 m) below the surface. Light cannot reach them, and the force of so much water around them produces pressure that would crush most submarines. Examples include the black devilfish (top left), a bathypelagic (deep-sea) lizard fish, and a footballfish (bottom).

Marine·PACIFIC OCEAN

THE BIG BLUE

The Pacific is the largest of the world's seven oceans. Its waters stretch from pole to pole and from Asia to the Americas. With that much ocean, it's not surprising that an incredible diversity of marine life lives there. Most of the animals people are familiar with live along the coastlines of countries bordering the ocean as well as around the thousands of islands in the Pacific, but some really amazing creatures live in the deepest part of this deepest ocean.

PACIFIC OCEAN

HUMPBACK WHALE

Of the dozens of whale species that swim the world's oceans, humpback whales take some of the longest trips. Examples of their migration routes go back and forth from the Equator to the South Pole or from the cold waters around Alaska to warmer seas near Mexico. Along the way, they eat tons of tiny crustaceans called krill.

GLOSSARY

adapted changed habits over time to become more suited to living in a certain place

amphibian an animal that can live on land and in the water

arachnid an arthropod that has eight legs

brood a group of baby birds or reptiles

carcass the body of a dead animal

carnivore an animal that eats meat

> I'm a carnivore. I'm also a scavenger, looking for carcasses when I forage!

conservation the practice of working to make sure that animals, plants, and the environment are kept safe for the future

elevations levels of the land above sea level; higher ones are in mountains

endangered a label given to animal species that are in danger of becoming extinct

evolved changed the structure of an animal or plant over a long period of time to become better at surviving

food web a pattern of animals who depend on one another for food. Food webs are made up of many food chains.

forage to search for food on land

habitat the place where an animal lives

herbivore an animal that eats only plants

hibernation a period of deep, sleep-like rest that animals enter to make it safely through harsh winters

insect a type of arthropod with six legs and an exoskeleton, and (usually) wings

invertebrate an animal without a spine

mammal a warm-blooded animal that has fur or hair and feeds milk to its young

marsupial a mammal that carries its young in an external pouch

metamorphose change, usually from one life stage of an animal to another

> You're looking at an animal that has finished metamorphosizing!

migration a journey an animal makes to move from one habitat to another; usually a long journey made each year

omnivore an animal that eats both plants and meat

pampas a South American name for grasslands

poaching the unauthorized and illegal killing of wild animals

raptor a bird of prey, such as an eagle or hawk

rodent a mammal that has two larger front teeth it uses for biting

salinity a measure of how salty water is

scavenger an animal that eats dead animals

temperate having generally mild temperatures year-round

tentacles long, arm-like body parts such as those of jellyfish or octopuses

treaties agreements between nations intended to solve or prevent problems

tree line the area on a rising mountainside beyond which trees and large vegetation cannot grow due to weather or altitude

zooplankton tiny or even microscopic animals that live in the sea

ANIMAL INDEX

This list includes all the animals mentioned inside. The continent chapters are in bold.

PHOTO CREDITS

bkgd: background. DT: Dreamstime.com; SS: Shutterstock.com;
DP: Dollar Photo Club; NPL: Nature Picture Library

COVERS
Henner Damke/DT (jaguar); Witr/DT (bkgd fur); Nick Garbutt/NPL (spider monkey); Dennis Jacobsen/DTe (macaw) Dannyphoto80/Dreamstime (cobra); Isselee/DT (koala); Howard Cheek/DT (cardinal).

INTRODUCTION
Exorzist/SS (panda); Sumiphoto/DT (rabbit); Pavel Lipsky/DT (alpine); Nikolay Stanev/DT (desert); Marc Witte/DT (marine); Issellee/DT (grass); Mathes/DT (rainforest); Rinus Baak/DT (forest); Chris Boswell/DT (taiga); Yurataranik/DT (tundra).

ASIA
10-11: Peter Wollinga/DT (bkgd); Kjorgen/DT (orangutan); Photomaru/DT (dragon); Pe3k/SS (insect); Warmer/SS (loris); FLPA/Superstock (frog); Mark Carwardine/NPL (rhino). 12-13: Patryk Kosmider/DT (bkgd); Craig Burrows/SS (cobra); Michael Ninger/SS (gibbon); Chienphotospirit/DT (centipede); Tim Lamen/NGC/NPL (bird); Smellme/DT (monkey); Palangsi/DT (snake); Akiyoko/SS (spider). 14-15: Michael Knitl/DT (bkgd); Kjorgen/DT (panda); Mikelane45/DT (bird); Andrey Zudillin/DT (lizard); John Braid/DT (bharal); Yongyat Kumsri/SS (bharal inset); Samrat35/DT (yak); Pod6666/DT (snow leopard). 16-17: Hecke01/DT (bkgd); Digitalimagined/DT (lizard); Mgkuijpers/DT (jerboa); Rune Mitgaard (gecko); Postalyon/DT (hunter); Martin Applegate/DT (eagle); Wimclaes/DT (fox). 18-19: Erinpackardphotography/DT (bkgd); Scherbinator/DT (saiga); Exorzist/SS (panda); Hanne and Jens Eriksen/NPL (lapwing); Sandesh Kudar/NPL (hog); Vladimir Michael Kogen/SS (eagle). 20: Qin0377/DT (bkgd); Sergey Gorshkov/NPL (sable); John Braid/DT (goral); Lukas Blazek/DT (pheasant); Sleiselei/DT (crane). 21: V450505/DT (bkgd); Fingers234/DT (duck); Moori/DT (reindeer); Mirceax/DT (owl); Jeanninebryan/DT (moose). 22: Scheriton/DT (main); Kellers/DT (inset).

AFRICA
26-27: Andrewro/DT (bkgd); Ingo Rechenberg (Cebrennus rechenbergi, spider); Riaanvdb/DT (bird); Smellme/DT (addax); Mgkuipiers/DT (snake); Arnoud Quanjer (lizard); Laborant/SS (camel head); Ealisa/DT (camel). 28-29: Niserin/DT (bkgd); Nico Smit/DT (lion and rhino); Satara910 (hippo); Lucasdm/SS (cheetah); Jabruson/NPL (python). 30-31: Alextara/DT (bkgd); Fouroaks/DT (beetle and giraffe); Mattiaath/DT (zebra); Charlie Summers/NPL (turtle); Louis Viatour (crane); Nataliya Hora/DT (shoebill); Nico Smit (ostrich); Byrdyak/DT (wildebeest). 32-33: Jalvarezg/DP (bkgd); Stuart Key/DT (gorilla); Mikdam/DT (parrot); Visual Unlimited/NPL (ants); Mgkuipers/DT (lizard); Eric Gaeevert/SS (lemurs); Warwick Slos/NPL (mosquito). 34-35: Sergey Uryadnikov/SS (shark); Joe Quinn/SS (turtle); Criminalatt/DT (bass); Frantisekhojdysz/SS (reef); Awiebadenhorst/DT (lobster); Allnaturalbeth/DT (tuna). 36-37: Starper/DT (main); Anup Shah/Nature Picture Library (inset).

EUROPE
40-41: Stevanzz/DT (bkgd); Wild Wonders of Europe/NPL (bustard); Dmytro Pylypenko/DT (falcon); Diversitystudio1/DT; Hector Ruiz Vilar/SS (snake); Jürgen Berger/Max Planck Institute for Developmental Biology (nematode); Lukas Blazek/DT (fish). 42-43: Wojphoto/DT (bkgd); Milous Chab/DT (bison); Jurra8/DT (kestrel); Ian Recchio (snake); Belizar/DT (beetle); Pyshnyy Maxim Vjacheslavovich/SS (toad); Neil Burton/DT (squirrel); KDemian/SS (badger). 44-45: Lfyv75/DT (bkgd); Photographerlondon/DT (marmot); DrPantaleon (salamander); Lues01/DT (bird); Thomasamm/DT (butterfly); Gaschwald/DT (ibex). 46-47: Wladbvbh/DT (bkgd); Baardema/DT (ermine); Eric Medard/NPL (bat); Peter Wey/SS (hare); Jouni Koskela (seal); Diego Delso (elephant rock); Pavel Svoboda/DT (puffin); Mikelane45/DT (swan). 48-49: CreativeNature R. Zwerver/SS (main); Igos/DT (inset).

NORTH AMERICA
52-53: Ritu Jethani/DT (bkgd); Mary Terriberry/SS (cicada); Ian Recchio (toad); David Coleman/DT (raccoon); Darren Hedges/DT (squirrel); Yevgenia Gorbulsky/123RF (falcon); Howard Cheek/DT (bird); Matt Jepson/SS (snake); Gonepaddling/DT (deer). 54-55: Meinzahn/DT (bkgd); Steven Johnson (dragonfly); Wolfgang Kaehler/ Getty Images (glass frog); Nicholashan/DT (beetle); Bence Mate/NPL (lizard); Henner Damke/DT (jaguar); Hangitshop/DT (macaw). 56-57: Vladislav Gajic/DT (bkgd); Alpstraum/DT (bison); Americanspirit/DT (dog); Dan Cardiff/iStock (hawk); Steve Byland/DT (bird); Gregory Gendusa/DT (snake); Abesolom Zerit/DT (grasshopper). 58-59: Kkistl01/DT (bkgd); IrinaK/SS (scorpion); Rafael Arroyo Argudo/DT (eagle); Ian Recchio (snake); Sumikphoto/DT (rabbit); Mgkuijpers/DT (Gila monster); Sekar B/SS (bird); Tarsal Claw/SS (wasp). 60: Pilens/DT (bkgd); Lynn Bystrom/iStock (bear); Michael Ninger/SS (wolverine); Wildphotos/DT (salamander); David Cutts/DT (bird). 61: Alexsandr Frolov/DT (bkgd); James Pintar/DT (owl); Emi/SS (fox); Outdoorsman/SS (bears); Vladimir Melnik/SS (walrus). 62: Danielle Heskamp/DT (eagle). 63: Michael Robbins/DT (inset).

SOUTH AMERICA
66-67: Salparadis/DT (bkgd); Lightpoet/SS (monkey); Pablo Hidalgo/DT (tapir); Pedro Bernardo/SS (bat); worldswildlifewonders/SS (otter); Scanrail/DT (toucan); Vilainecrevette/DT (sloth). 68-69: Strixcode/DT (bkgd); Rafael Ben-Ari/DT (snake); Michaelmajor/DT (piranha circle); Kosmos111/DT (piranha); Mgjukipers/DT (spider); Toniflap/DT (caiman); Pete Oxford/NPL (lizard); Ginosphotos/DT (blue morpho); Wansfordphoto/SS (glasswing); Atelopus/DT (rionid). 70-71: Kovgabor79/DT (bkgd); Elnavagente/DT (hummingbird); Bert Wilaeert/NPL (toad); Su Oken/Wikimedia (tamarin); Stubblefield Photography/SS (woodpecker); Jose Luis Bartheldi/Flickr (monito); Virgonira/DT (pudu). 72-73: rm/SS (bkgd); Ondrej Prosicky/SS (armadillo); Rod Williams/NPL (cat); Prillfoto/DT (rhea); Jocrebbin/DT (stork); Paulo Resende/DT (capybara); Lukas Blazek/DT (wolf). 74: Fabio Lamanna/DP (bkgd); Roland Seitre/NPL (viscacha); Gerd Huedepohl (lizard); Jeff McGraw/SS (flamingo); Chbaum/DT (penguin). 75: Angela Ostafichuk/DT (bkgd); Ian Recchio (anole); Alessandro Catenazzi (frog); Mirmoor/DT (llama); Iakov Fillimonov/SS (condor). 76: Joelfotos/DT (main); Vadim Petrakov/DT (inset).

AUSTRALIA
80: Inavanhateren/DT (bkgd); Michael Ninger/SS (kookaburra); Curioso/SS (emu); Reg Morrison/Minden Pictures (spider); John Carnemolla/SS (dingo). 81: Joseph Gough/DT (bkgd); Marco Tomasini/DT (wombat); Robert Valentic/Nature Picture Library (dragon); Tonympix/DT (bird); Hotshotsworldwide/DT (koala). 82-83: Ross Kummer/DT (bkgd) Tanya Puntii/SS (beaked coralfish); Whitcomberd/DT (turtle); Hubkp0a1/DT (croc); Sebastian Burel/SS (clam); Reinhard Dirscherl/ullstein bild via Getty Images (whale shark); Henner Damke/SS (foxface and angelfish); Ian Scott/SS (idol). 84: Eduard Kyslynskyy/SS (main); Veroxdale/SS (inset).

ANTARCTICA
88: Slew11/DT (bkgd); Norbert Wu/Minden Pictures (dragonfish); Norbert Wu/Minden Pictures (worms); Dmytro Pylypenko/DT (seal). 89: Staphy/DT (albatross); Richard Lee (midge); Jocrebbin (seal). Brandon Smith/DT (penguin); Gentoomultimedia/DT (bkgd).

OCEANS
90-91: Natursports/DT (jelly); Amanda Nicholls/DT (ray); Peter Scoones/NPL (lobster); Allnaturalbeth/DT (flounder); Uwe Kils (amphipod and krill); David Shale/NPL (sea angel); Solvin Zanki/NPL (sea butterfly). 92-93: Solvin Zanki/NPL (dragonfish); David Shale/NPL (lizardfish); Doc White/NPL (footballfish) Michael Pitts/NPL (seahorse); Franco Balfi/NPL (sunfish); Cbpix/SS (clownfish); Andreistancu/DT (octopus); Yann Hubert/SS (whale).

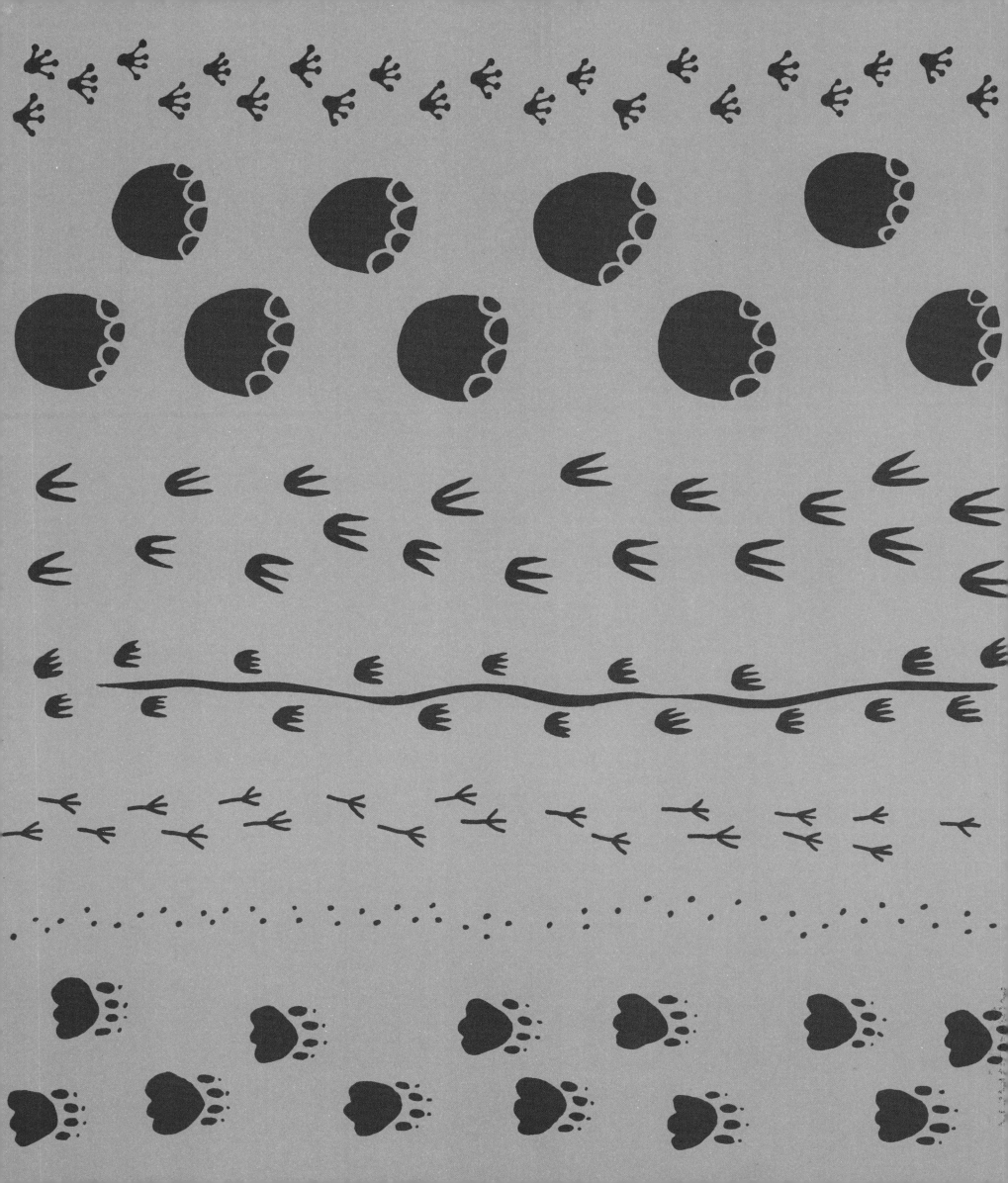